Praise for the new editio

With inspiring wisdom from the past and engaging contemporary insights, this most welcome volume boldly takes on the serious ecological challenges facing us today. The text is informed by evolutionary science, scriptural insight, and open-eyed social engagement. Each page is written with an evident spirit of deep concern for our fragile ecosystem and abiding compassion for all its inhabitants. The author's call for harmony, balance, peace, and care for the earth is exactly what we need to hear today: the message of geo-justice. This well-articulated vision of a healthier cosmos will allow all who read this book to grow in awareness of the sacredness of all creation and will energize us to work for a better world.

—**Thomas Massaro, S.J.,** Professor of Moral Theology, Jesuit School of Theology of Santa Clara University

Jim Conlon wrote this book with passion and intelligence. What a wonderful and rare combination! I assure you that you will be inspired—set aflame, actually—as I was by Jim's unsentimental, wise, and absolutely timely message. He writes as a theologian activist. I miss this important voice in the Catholic tradition: visionary, compassionate, earth-loving.

—**Thomas Moore,** author of *Care of the Soul*

To address our present ecological predicament, we need a new vision of the world and a creative new way of understanding our relationship to it. Conlon's compelling notion of geo-justice is not only indispensable to such a vision but also a prime candidate for becoming the operative myth for our time.

—**John F. Haught,** Professor Emeritus, Department of Theology, Georgetown University

Jim Conlon identified the needed linkage of ecology and justice twenty years ago. Now he is revisiting geo-justice through the lens of Pope Francis' encyclical, *Laudato Si'*. The result is a passionate book that needs to be read and put into practice by all who care about the future of our planet.

—**Mary Evelyn Tucker**, Yale Forum on Religion and Ecology

This is a book of depth and wisdom. Jim Conlon has been deeply engaged in the greening of the Earth for many years and this succinct work draws us into a new vision for a new world. With a poetic heart and searching mind, Jim is a seer and a prophet for our age. Read this book slowly and prayerfully, and you will awake to see the world in a new way.

—**Ilia Delio, OSF,** Villanova University

Geo-justice initiates a new context for theological discussion of justice issues. Gone forever are the former dualisms that pitted human social concerns on one side and environmental concerns on the other. Conlon establishes a holistic orientation that assists us in exploring the justice implications of one Earth, that helps us hold our minds open both to the beauty and the crisis of our time, and that enables us to articulate our deepest convictions and plan for action.

—**Brian Swimme,** co-author with Thomas Berry of *The Universe Story*

In this work, Jim Conlon unites prose, poetry, and prayer in a healing reflection on what humanity belongs to, and is called to strive toward and to celebrate. We encounter in this thoughtful exposition deep and challenging insights fueled by hope, courage, and profound wisdom—a graced vision!

—**Barbara Fiand,** SNDdeN

Trowbridge & Tintera Publishing
562 Winthrop Road
Union, NJ 07083

Printed in the United States of America

Conlon, Jim, 1936-
Geo-Justice: The Emergency of Integral Ecology
Print ISBN: 978-0-9964387-2-8
Ebook ISBN: 978-0-9964387-3-5

Geo-Justice

The Emergence of Integral Ecology

Jim Conlon

Trowbridge & Tintera Publishing
www.txt.buzz

Dedication

To Pope Francis

I thank you for creating a tone of mercy and compassion within the church and beyond. I am especially grateful for your description of environmental and social justice as one vision and one work of integral ecology, and the way in which evolutionary science is woven into your letter, Laudato Si', such that "the cry of the poor and the cry of the Earth" can be heard on every page. I celebrate how your love of the poor and the marginalized pulsates in your writing and your life. Like so many, I am stirred by your compassion and concern. Your call to people in their poverty and powerlessness reminds me of Jesus of Nazareth; in your wisdom, you remind all of us of the beauty of God's creation and that we are called to do marvelous things.

Contents

Foreword to the 2017 Edition
by Sean McDonagh, SSC
December 6, 2016

Jim Conlon's book, *Geo-Justice: The Emergence of Integral Ecology*, is published at an extraordinary time. In the United States, Donald Trump has been elected president after the most divisive campaign in modern U.S. history. Unfortunately, the impact of Donald Trump's election will be felt well beyond the shores of the United States. His environmental policies, and especially his spurious claims that climate change is a hoax, will make it much more difficult to reduce greenhouse gases globally. Failure to deal with climate change will mean more severe weather, droughts and floods, and rising sea levels. All of these are currently affecting the United States, but the most serious impact of climate change is in poor countries in Africa, Asia, and the Pacific.

Environmentalists and others were appalled that President-elect Trump named Myron Ebell of the business-backed Competitive Enterprise Institute to head his EPA transition team. In 2007, a *Vanity Fair* profile of Mr. Ebell called him the oil industry's mouthpiece.

But the nationalist/populist political rhetoric is not confined to the United States. It raised its ugly head in the Brexit vote in Britain in June 2016. Trump's victory can be seen as a harbinger of the far-right's prospects in France, the Netherlands, Germany, Austria, and Italy. Already populists are in power in Hungary and Poland, where they are introducing anti-immigration policies. At the same time, a vicious, bloody war is going on in Syria and Iraq, where it has claimed tens of thousands of lives. In the current political world order, no one seems to be able to stop or deal with the flood of refugees who are fleeing these conflicts.

Yet, there are also wonderful things happening across the globe. Conlon points to the election of Pope Francis in 2013, and to how quickly under his leadership, the Catholic Church, which had been fairly mute on environmental issues, began to address some of the most serious ecological issues across the globe. One direct result of Pope Francis's concerns for the poor and the Earth was the issuing of a groundbreaking encyclical entitled *Laudato Si': On Care for Our Common Home* in May 2015. In his book, Conlon teases out the various strands of what he calls "geo-justice" as it operates at the individual, social, and planetary levels. The dynamic transformation involved in geo-justice is a clear invitation to change the dominant narrative humans have of our relationship with ourselves, other humans, and the Earth. We are moving from a narrative of control and abuse to one of solidarity and communion.

Another sign of hope is the realization that many, many people are now highly critical of the destructive ways humans have related to each other and the Earth during the past two hundred years. Conlon witnessed many such transformations during his thirty years involved in social and ecological education at Holy Name University in Oakland, California. As a colleague, Brian Swimme, has written, Conlon saw students entering the program as members of an industrial society and leaving it transformed as "seed-bearers of a new planetary civilization."

In this exciting book, we have a distillation and an engaging presentation of Conlon's own educational journey over five decades. He had the privilege of working with some of the thoughtful and creative thinkers of the later part of the twentieth century. In the 1970s, he studied at Saul Alinsky's

Industrial Areas Foundation in Chicago. Like many of us who were working with oppressed communities, Conlon honed his approach to education with the insights of Brazilian educationalist Paulo Freire. According to Freire, education is not neutral. It can be used to domesticate people into believing that the status quo cannot be challenged or changed, or it can be used to liberate people and enable them to organize themselves and work against all forms of oppression and domination.

This focus on addressing and changing the social and community dimension of human culture was further widened and deepened when Conlon came in contact with the work and writings of Thomas Berry. In chapter 2 of this book, Conlon admits that before discovering Berry, his approach "to justice lacked a connection to the Earth." Conlon realized that his earlier engagement in community building and social organization lacked the dynamic focus that the cosmic story brings to integrating his personal, social, and global concerns. He points out that when people focused on personal transformation and those focused on social change work in isolation, and without understanding their place in the universe and what is happening to it, "each fails to encompass the wisdom available to the other. One pursues emotional healing while overlooking oppressive structures, and the other seeks systemic change without dealing with personal need."

For Conlon, geo-justice is the most holistic way of understanding the challenges facing us, our society, and our cosmic journey at this precise point in human history. We learn about our place in the universe both through the eyes of science and the Christian gospel: "Geo-justice brings a synthesis of socioeconomic concerns and ecological justice."

Some people who have been exposed to the extraordinary insights of Thomas Berry, based partly on the writing of Teilhard de Chardin, reject or forget their Christian past, with its rich biblical tradition. Conlon does not do this. He claims that "in the Cosmic Christ theology, we come to believe that the Christian story is identical with the universe story." He links the Trinitarian perspective with the fundamental dynamism of the cosmic story, as it reveals itself to us in the differentiation of all things that we experience in the cosmos, the interiority or inner dimension that each reality has, and the connectedness of everything in the universe.

Conlon keeps repeating that we are citizens of the Earth, and geo-justice challenges us to make "a preferential option for the Earth." Conlon would reject out of hand the Communion Prayer for Advent in the Pius V Roman Missal. It called on worshippers to "to reject the things of Earth and love the things of Heaven." I don't think he would applaud the horrible and incompetent recent translation of the Roman Missal, which encourages us to "judge wisely the things of Earth." Conlon is clear that "solidarity, in turn, helps us discover that the needs of the Earth are one with our own deepest desires." Our work or vocation as Earthlings is to bring "harmony and balance to the planet" wherever we live today.

Within the confines of this relatively slim book, Conlon deals with some of the most profound issues of our times. He shows us how not to succumb to despair, but to emerge transformed and victorious. The book could be very useful for community or parish groups who are striving to educate themselves about what is happening in our world in order to heal themselves, our society, and our planet.

Apart from his insights and the clarity of his writing, Conlon provides the reader with challenging questions. He asks us to discuss, for example, how we might "build mediating institutions between the powerful structures of greed that dominate our lives and the gentler forms designed for nature?"

Finally, Conlon tells us that, "For the new era of global interdependence, we need a mature spirituality that reverences creation for its own sake, a spirituality that understands our perception of creation through the senses as an experience of the divine. We need to be able to deal with social structures as well as personal attitudes, with multinational corporations as well as family life. For we are dealing here with our whole civilization, our whole planet."

Given the difficult times we are entering with the Trump presidency and right-wing, nationalist and populist rhetoric spreading across the globe, many groups will value a book such as Conlon's, that focuses on the real world and how we might make it a more just and compassionate place.

Foreword to the First Edition
by Thomas Berry, C.P., Ph.D.
1990

This book by James Conlon might be considered something of a flowering of the ecology movement which began with Rachel Carson's *Silent Spring*, published in 1962. Since then an ever-increasing transformation of human consciousness has been taking place. It is the most significant transformation movement, perhaps, since the beginning of civilization.

Some 5,000 years ago, humans began putting stress upon the natural world that has culminated in the industrial assault on the planet in these past two centuries. This final assault originated in the Western European world, then extended to North America and throughout the planet. Its most obvious example is the petrochemical industry of the post-war period, an industry that has multiplied itself and is now in its most virulent phase.

Resistance to the disturbed relations between humans and the Earth was begun in the 19th century, but this movement was overwhelmed by the power of the commercial-industrial enterprise, and by the mystique of "progress" that has pervaded all our thinking, our education, and our sense of reality and value. But now, finally, after *Silent Spring*, a tide of opposition has arisen. Our industrial "progress" is now recognized as a deep cultural pathology that has poisoned our environment and given us a grimy world.

The ecology movement began a profound cultural therapy. It seeks not the exploitation of the Earth but a mutually enhancing human presence on the Earth. This movement is guided by an awareness that the universe is a communion of subjects, not a collection of objects. But if this is true of the universe, it is infinitely more true of the Earth in its myriad expressions of geological, biological, and human modes of being and acting.

For too long we have been autistic in relation to the natural world. We did not hear the voices, we did not experience the exaltation of speaking and listening to the mountains, the rivers, the meadows, the birds, the cicadas and crickets on summer evenings. It was all lovely enough, entrancing as the sea in all its power and majesty as we walk along the shore. But all these experiences were trivial in their impact on human consciousness; they did not prevent us from our ever-increasing devastation.

Finally, however, we have entered on a new period. Naturalists such as Loren Eiseley have restored the natural history essay that had such wonderful expression in the 19th century. The archetypal figures will always be Henry Thoreau and John Muir, but new writers such as Peter Matthiesson, Farley Mowat, David Raines Wallace, Scott Momaday, Barry Lopez and Annie Dillard, and poets such as Gary Snyder and Wendell Berry, now present us with remarkable insight into the experiences of the plant and animal realms. Such writers are joined by scientists and others on ecological issues—along with an extensive array of publications from eco-feminists, religious authors, and those concerned with ethical aspects of the environmental issue.

Within this context, we can see this book on geo-justice as a flowering of the entire movement.

The full power of ecology can only be felt in the realization that the universe, the planet Earth, and all living and non-living beings exist primarily for celebration. The universe is a single, vast, celebratory event! Here the poetry, the music, the mystique of the Earth—all find expression. Just as the earliest of the natural history writers were inspired by the romantic tradition of the later 18th century and the beginning of the 19th century, so now after a period of "realism" that had no place for the more numinous qualities of the universe we are able once again to hear the music and experience the depth of fulfillment that are available to us, once we are attuned to the symphony of voices around us.

An Ode to Integral Ecology

Ancient One,
source of far-off days,
I celebrate your great, refreshing gift.

Born from the womb
of a holistic worldview,
you hold creation together
in one compassionate embrace,
a synthesis of humanity and Earth,
a luscious garden of beauty,
in which all the elements were formed.

Brother Sun, Sister Moon,
we are all cosmic beings,
focused and formed in the
great flaring forth.

Born of the cosmic mystery
in the heart of God,
we are one family of life,
cousin and kin to the stars, mountains,
antelopes and sheep.
We gather together
on this great, gorgeous planet.

We've always belonged
to this planet
we call home.

Preface to the New Edition

We live in a busy, often restless world. Much of what we see and experience around us—and even within us—seems incomprehensible.

Yet, many of us feel called to a greater destiny, to solve the problems we see, however insurmountable they may appear at this moment in Earth/human history. And so we search. We look up into the sky and into the depths of our psyches. Insight flashes, and our horizon widens. Slowly our vision expands to reveal a vast cosmic perspective.

Down the hall in the apartment building where I live in Berkeley is a baby girl. Whenever I hear her in her carriage as her parents take her for a walk, I am comforted by the gurgling, childlike sounds she makes. When I hear her song, I say to myself it is the sound of vitality, fresh energy, and new life. This little one is well on her way to giving expression to the divine energy that will give shape and form to her life as the years go by.

The trajectory of this energy as it unfolds in the months and years to come can be understood as her *spirituality*. As she grows and matures, we can predict that she will be comforted by love, challenged by pain, and encouraged by acts of creativity and compassion. In the days ahead, she undoubtedly will experience deep longings in her heart as she explores relationships with those with whom she shares a common home, and later with those she encounters as she walks through the world. In life, she will inevitably be touched by mystery, by a sense of the sacred. She may strive to come to terms with that holy mystery. She may choose to name it as the divine, God, or simply as an invisible presence she perceives.

Like this young child, we are challenged at this cultural moment to learn about, better understand, cherish, and ultimately save the world in which we live. Much of what was taken for granted by previous generations can no longer be ignored. We no longer have such a luxury. This is a critical time for Earth and its people. Therefore, we seek and continue to pray, hoping that some day, out of the fog of uncertainty and doubt, will emerge a new clarity and direction for the days ahead.

Cultural movements, like waves upon the shore of life, rise and fall, only to rise again. We have arrived at a time that is unique in the intensity of its challenge. It is a time to witness the melting away of static beliefs, and reconcile our experience of contemporary culture with our understanding of the revealed word of our Christian faith. It is a time to affirm our notion of God as holy mystery, to experience the divine presence while we become fully engaged in the great dramas of ecological devastation and human poverty. It is a time when a new wave of engagement calls us into action.

I call this movement *geo-justice*.

Geo-justice is a vision that brings the human, the Earth, the universe, and the divine into a profound immediacy with each other. It is a process to re-imagine the world as we would like it to be, and to take concrete steps to make that possible. Geo-justice is a journey that takes us to the far reaches of the universe and returns us to each new moment, in which we become agents of transformation.

The original edition of this book was published in 1990. Unfortunately, in the quarter century that has passed since then, many of the social and ecological issues I wrote about have become increasingly dire. For example, global warming has continued and even accelerated, with fifteen of the sixteen hottest years on record falling within the current century, while sea ice levels are at record lows. The United Nations has estimated people are being displaced as a result of climate-related disasters at the rate of one person every second. This does not include the tens of millions who are being forced to flee their homelands because of political conflict and humanitarian crises. At the same time, however, we have new cause for hope. Foremost in this respect are the words and mission of Pope Francis. In his encyclical *Laudato Si': On Care for our Common Home*, published in May 2015, he calls for a dynamic integration of social and ecological concerns, which he refers to as *integral ecology.*

Pope Francis is the first pope to emphasize the ecological devastation taking place on our planet, including global warming, sea level rise, decreasing crop yields, flooding and drought, water scarcity, extinction of species, illness caused by polluted water and toxic lands, and the impact of all of these on our livelihoods and on survival itself. He calls for us to care for our common home and to nurture a new consciousness, as well as a culture of dialogue and inclusion that can heal what ails our world.

This is a sacred moment in history, a turning point for the church and people of God. It is a time such as I have not experienced since the pontificate of St. John XXIII and the amazing events during and following the Second Vatican Council.

According to Mary Evelyn Tucker and John Grim of Yale University's Forum on Religion and Ecology, "While discussions about social justice have been robust in Catholic and Christian contexts, this encyclical marks the first time social and environmental concerns are brought together." Today, Christians are challenged to create a new vision of the world that will make it possible to listen deeply to the "cry of the earth and the cry of the poor" and respond. To enact this vision requires that we penetrate the blindness of injustice, allow the veil of darkness to be lifted, and engage together in social and ecological acts of communion and compassion.

As I closely studied and reflected upon Pope Francis's message in light of the challenges before us, I felt moved to revise the earlier edition, *Geo-Justice: A Preferential Option for the Earth*. In this work, I focused on the meaning of justice and the need for harmony, balance, and peace for the planet and the people. The theme of the book remains the same, a reflection of the fact that the basic problems have yet to be solved. I have also incorporated updated information and have added a new, timelier perspective, inspired by my contemplation of Pope Francis's teachings.

A focus of this new edition is what I refer to as *the gospel of the moment*. I speak of this in the first section of the book as the urgent call we cannot ignore, and I discuss the need for an operative theology to guide our work. The final section of the book presents what I call the gospel of the moment process, through which we are empowered to explore avenues of engagement that speak to the deepest recesses of our lives and give voice to our longing for a world of harmony, balance, and peace.

—**Jim Conlon**, December 2016

PART I
Justice for the Earth

Chapter 1
Gospel of the Moment

The rich heritage of Christian spirituality, the fruit of twenty centuries of personal and communal experience, has a precious contribution to make to the renewal of humanity…The teachings of the Gospel have direct consequences for our way of thinking, feeling and living.
— **Pope Francis** (*Laudato Si'*, 216)

For many years I have lived in the San Francisco Bay Area, which is well known for its progressive culture, and for the many programs based here dedicated to uplifting the poor and saving the Earth. One such program is St. Mary's Center, a courageous beacon of light in Oakland that offers a better, healthier life to the homeless, recovery for the addicted, and food for the hungry. Another project is the Ecology Center in Berkeley, which for decades has been a resource for a broad spectrum of ecological concerns, including making wholesome food available through community-supported agriculture and farmers' markets. Yes, good work—both social and ecological—continues to take place in Oakland and Berkeley, and in many others towns and cities around the country and beyond, as well.

There is a long and noble Catholic tradition focused on the care of the poor, homeless, and hungry. Religious communities of women, especially, have dedicated their lives to the care of the "anawim"—the most poor, the powerless, and those without a voice in society. A response to the cry of the Earth has been a less significant priority for most Catholics. However, in recent years, a few voices have begun to arise. Fr. Thomas Berry, CP, priest and scholar of cultural history, sought to bridge the divide we have maintained between the human and other-than-human worlds. With a courageous and prophetic voice, he proclaimed, "You can't have healthy people on a sick planet."

Berry's often quoted phrase, "the universe is a communion of subjects, not a collection of objects," speaks directly to his vision of an integral ecology. In this statement, he emphasizes how we exist in relationship with the Earth, as people of the Earth, and stresses the depths and interconnection in all our relationships. This spiritual-physical communion can be understood as foundational for integral ecology. Berry writes, "The integral ecologist can now be considered a normative guide for our times.... The integral ecologist is the spokesperson for the planet."

Another leading voice is that of Leonardo Boff. In *The Cry of the Earth, the Cry of the Poor,* he unites his concern for those overwhelmed by poverty in the barrios of Brazil with his concern for the parched, arid lands of his home country. The first to use the term integral ecology in print, he writes about the need to connect our spiritual vision with the needs of the people and the planet.

I see the work of Berry and Boff as foundational to the vision of integral ecology named by Pope Francis in his letter to the world, *Laudato Si'*. In this encyclical, he writes, "We are faced not with two separate crises, one environmental and the other social, but rather with one complex crisis which is both social and environmental." And he says, "A true ecological approach always becomes a social approach... so as to hear both the cry of the earth and the cry of the poor."

Integral ecology implies a departure from the prior emphasis on social over ecological concerns and instills a new relationship between society and nature that will result in the preservation of life as we know it. This is an issue we can no longer ignore. Integral ecology must serve as our gospel of the moment.

Our Great Story

At the heart of integral ecology is the principle of geo-justice. Geo-justice is born out of the deep and vast cosmic womb that flared forth 14 billion years ago and continues to unfold. Out of that original ignition of cosmic energy, the galaxies were formed and the elements came into being; eventually, the planets appeared, including planet Earth. Following an extended transformational period, about 550 million years ago, life appeared on the Earth; plants and animals came into existence. As one chapter of this great story, about 26 million years ago, humans emerged to walk on this Earth.

At this culminating phase of our story, we are able to discover our place in a vast universe. The story of the unfolding universe can be understood as also the story of humanity. In the words of Thomas Berry and Brian Thomas Swimme, we celebrate the realization that "there is eventually only one story, the story of the universe." This is a story to be celebrated in music, art, poetry, ritual, prayer and spiritual practice.

We move forward, energized by the evolving universe and the meaning of existence. We seek a new synthesis that perceives God as a compassionate presence, the source from which to activate the cosmic energies to heal what is broken and renew the face of the Earth. We become justice makers for the Earth and all creation, as each member of the Earth community becomes engaged in this vast evolutionary process to inaugurate a new horizon of hope. This hope is infused with a fresh energy, derived from the wisdom of the universe, the depths of our religious traditions, and a profound sense of compassion.

We have entered a new era; we have before us a new story of geo-justice. We reflect on the transformational moments that have brought us to this moment and that reveal a sense of the sacred. The traditional approaches of theology and philosophy remain as true as before, yet they tend to be downplayed in this scientific era. We are guided by a scientific understanding about how the universe began and the formation of the planets, life, and the human. If we are to have an adequate understanding of God, I believe it must be congruent with the understanding available to us through science. This becomes possible—as we shall discover in the chapters that follow—when we study geo-justice as a reflection of the three dynamic principles of the universe.

Giving Birth to our Future

The challenges of the future are many. Ecological devastation, the extinction of species, drug abuse, the fate of the poor, gun violence, world hunger—all these and more demand our attention. Geo-justice, more broadly grasped, offers a new language and a new approach that seeks to put these problems into a unified context for protecting the planet and transforming human culture. In geo-justice, we understand the principle of interconnectedness, whereby working on one problem synergistically contributes to work on other problems, and to the healing of the whole.

Geo-justice is born out of the quest for a vision that can give guidance and meaning to our lives. At this defining moment in human/Earth history, we are beginning to see the world differently. We are exploring a new way of being in the world: a new way to observe the world, to deepen our awareness, and to pray and act in response to the great challenges before us. We have arrived at a new moment of religious sensitivity that calls forth from humanity a new story; new dreams; new responses in art, music, prayer, and poetry, and new and integral approaches to challenging the social and ecological issues that confront us.

We cannot be tricked into forgetting that there is profound goodness in life. This goodness shows up in the banquet of beauty that surrounds us. The rich cultural diversity of the peoples of the Earth is itself a banquet. So is the gentle strength of prophets, saints, and anyone who gives voice to the voiceless, roofs to the homeless, and hospitality to all who would join an ever-increasing circle of hope and engagement.

Celebrating this goodness, we take a stand against and work to dissolve the institutionalized violence expressed in racism, sexism, classism, and other isms. We honor our ancestors, upon whose shoulders we stand. Some years ago, I met an aboriginal teacher named Eddie Kneebone. A statement he made has stayed with me until today: "When I look at the stars at night, I believe I am seeing the bonfires of my ancestors." We acknowledge ancient wisdom and the roots of our tradition. We find the newness of the divine child in each beginning, and his tenderness and compassion at the crescendo and culmination of life.

History's unfolding provides us with an evolutionary consciousness. We look back over the centuries, and we see that time and again, humanity has faced specific problems and solved them. Yet now, the magnitude of the crises before us is so great that the outcome appears uncertain. When children live in fear because they don't know the security of a homeland, something must be fixed. When people in China have to stay indoors or must walk the streets with masks to protect themselves from pollution, it is obvious that something must be done, and soon. Yet, these are not just local or national problems. The atmosphere is not confined by boundaries. It requires a global movement, and swift action at all levels. It depends on a common vision, and our ability to carry that forth together.

We are called to give birth to the future in a way that humanity has never before confronted. Our very future is in question. To secure it, we must begin with the awareness that we are the Earth, and we are called to heal the planet.

The Resounding Call

Geo-justice is a resounding call to resacralize the Earth. Historically, the Christian vocation has often been stated as the urge and the need to "get back to Eden." Thus misguided, we lead our lives in a way that makes the garden the goal of life. Influenced by the creation story in the Book of Genesis, we believe that the meaning of life is to be found through focusing on the afterlife.

At a deep level, we are influenced by the image of the garden. Even the rugs in some homes are manufactured to resemble a garden. Indeed, we live oblivious to the needs of the present-day human and other-than-human worlds. This is a profoundly static vision of a mechanical world created and ruled by a transcendent God. According to this worldview, we see God as "up there," somehow distant and absent. This approach to the divine is known as *theism*, a notion of God that is removed from human experience.

Geo-justice embraces a different notion of divinity. This perspective is called *panentheism*. It is commonly expressed as "God in all things, all things in God." Medieval mystic

Mechthild of Magdeburg put it well when she wrote, "The day of my spiritual awakening was the day I saw and knew I saw all things in God and God in all things."

Based on this perspective, we are able to see that every molecule of existence is sacred and infused with divine presence. When we view the divine in this way and embrace an evolutionary world, we begin to shift our understanding from a static view of the world to an evolutionary view in which the divine is drawing us forward into the future. We understand that our vocational destiny is to resacrilize the Earth.

With Rabbi Abraham Heschel, we experience the intimate, divine presence and sensitivity to all creation. He writes, "Every time someone suffers, God cries."

We become aware of the extinction spasms that ravage the Earth and diminish our experience of beauty. When a species becomes extinct, we experience a loss—whether it is through the song of a bird, the beauty of a flower, the dance of a fish. The extinction of a species can be compared to the tearing of a page from sacred scripture.

Geo-justice is a resounding alarm to listen to the cry of the Earth. When we listen deeply, we are able to bring our awareness to the melting ice caps of the far North, the loss of half of the planet's topsoil over the past 150 years, and the paling of the human spirit.

When we reflect on the sanctity of our world, we are challenged to explore how the desacralizing of the Earth can render our lives less hopeful and diminish our vitality. With this in mind, questions arise:

- What is the significance of a baptism performed with polluted water?
- How can we be blessed by Eucharistic bread baked

from toxic wheat?

- Can we really talk meaningfully about salvation if we are not aware of the ecological devastation occurring around us?

Realizing the dynamic integration of ecology and social justice, we conclude there is a deep connection between the planet and its people. Geo-justice and integral ecology presuppose a profound interrelationship that calls us to cherish, nurture, and protect the Earth and everything—human and other than human—that exists upon it.

We visualize a melding of what were previously understood as polarities. Among these are theory and practice, man and woman, humanity and God. With this integrating vision, we embrace what we previously experienced as the fragmentation of our lives. When we look over the past, it is clear that each event, when properly reflected on, has brought us to a time of new beginnings and new hope.

When I came to California's shores more than twenty-five years ago to study and work in the area of culture and creation spirituality, it was in many ways a different time. The womb of the world's Abrahamic religions was boiling over in conflict and the insurgency of war. Today, that strife continues in the Middle East and elsewhere. Only the form of the battle and some of its players have changed.

In the intervening years, the world became more digitalized. Some have prospered, while many more have faced the increasingly wide separation between the affluent and the marginalized. This separation will only increase as low-lying areas of the planet become flooded, turning millions of the poor and marginalized into environmental refugees. In this defining moment, we witness a stirring in the hearts of people, particularly those who have felt and will feel the impact of diminished influence and increased insecurity about their future. With the swirl of time, dreams have been shattered and aspirations for a better tomorrow dashed.

Yet a constant cry echoes from the soul of the people. It was and continues to be a cry for recognition—a cry to be heard over the incessant noise of media, the silence of broken dreams, and despair.

Some of the cries that echo from the streets of today are:

"Black lives matter"
"One person, one vote"
"Raise the minimum wage"
"Affordable housing"
"Health care for all"
"#NoDAPL"
"Pure air, water, and land"
"Reduce the carbon footprint"
"Right to life for everyone—human and other than human
"Not my president"

In the midst of this time of turmoil and destruction, an enduring flame burns in the human heart. It is an energy that ignites the fire of engagement, that fuels the call for a better tomorrow.

As a new defining moment crests upon the shores of our era, we hear the call to geo-justice resounding from the cry of the people and the cry of the Earth. In fact, this call has been building for the past quarter century, or longer. It has reached such a pitch that we can no longer deny it. It has become our gospel of the moment.

This cry carries the melody of what is possible. Its lyrics are a message for people who are gathered in every corner of the world, with the will to listen and the fortitude to hope. The call of geo-justice is a song for all who would reclaim the soul of the people and the soul of the planet.

When we listen to the pulse of the people and the planet, we experience a heartbeat of hope. It is a clarion call to justice, a canticle arising from the recesses of the Earth and the people. It is a call to include the outsider, to sing a song of peace, to weave a quilt of compassion and a tapestry of wisdom, to issue a proclamation of freedom. It is a cry to heal the growing chasm between those who profit from the economic benefits of an unjust system and those who sink into poverty and cry out for change.

A geo-justice that is mystical and prophetic invites us into the great adventure that awaits—an exultation of existence that converges in a common destiny.

Process Reflection: Your Story

Speaking of the universe story, Thomas Berry says, "If you do not know the story, in a sense you do not know yourself; you do not know anything." The universe story becomes truly meaningful when we understand how our own stories relate to the greater whole. We see how the universe story is both sacred and scientific, both vast and personal. In this exercise, take some time to reflect on your own story and that of your ancestors. This exercise can be done alone or in a group.

1. Reflect on your own story—your early life, your current narrative, and your sense of the future. How does your story resonate with the call to geo-justice?

2. Reflect on the stories of you parents, grandparents, and the generations as far back as you know. What values, vision, and struggle did your ancestors bring to this planet? What implications do you see for your life today?
3. What stories have you heard, told, and lived that have altered your consciousness and connected you to the sacredness of life?
4. What aspects of your own story or your family's story call for your response at this defining moment in history?

Process Reflection: The Cosmic Walk

Through the ritual of the cosmic walk, reflect together on how your individual unfolding stories have deepened your understanding of the universe story. This reflection is done in a small group.

1. Take a long piece of colored yarn or cord and arrange it in the form of a spiral in the center of the room.
2. Each person places a candle at the center and at several intervals along the spiral, indicating the major phases of his or her unfolding story.
3. One by one, each participant walks into the spiral and lights his or her candles in sequence, announcing what that particular moment in time signifies for that person's story.
4. When each participant has reached the center, in silence, he or she takes the cosmic walk from the center back to the group.
5. When each participant completes the walk, the other members of the group proclaim, "The universe celebrates (name)."

Discovery

I want to tell you about discovery,
tell you about who I am,
about what I believe,
about faith, about justice,
about what I hope to say—
whether you believe it or not.

Justice is all I have to say.
When you tell me about sorrow and joy,
about the wound inside,
about organizing as your first act,
about recognizing others,
justice is all I have to say.

Justice making creates good companions
who eat common bread,
consume the food of freedom,
celebrate what is not to be found in books,
peer into silence and solitude.

Discover the wilderness
you dare to call your life.
Describe the scribe of your spirit,
the spirit who guides your uncertain pen
and reveals secrets yet untold.

Chapter 2
A New Planetary Paradigm

Each great turn of history introduces a new paradigm. This means that new forms of perceiving and interpreting reality emerge, that we are obliged to redefine the fundamental concepts that orient our social and personal lives including our concepts of God, human beings, history, the meaning of existence, and the universe.

—**Leonardo Boff** (foreword to *From the Stars to the Street*, 2007)

Let me offer a diagnosis of the problem. Until recently, justice work in our culture and our churches has lacked a connection with the Earth. In *The Culture of Narcissism*, Christopher Lasch was among the first to name our era as one in which preoccupation with self and introspection take precedence over communal instincts. Society fosters an ethos of individualism, whereby preoccupation with personal healing outweighs concerns for systemic change and transformation. We live in a new age of anxiety, as Thomas Berry once said, in which young people despair for the future.

In this book, I propose that justice in and through the Earth implies a transformation of people, society, and the planet. Like a hologram, in which any part of the picture can generate the whole image, each individual person represents all of society and the Earth. Therefore, we must work to transform all levels—personal, local, global—interdependently and simultaneously.

Geo-justice re-envisions justice making. In our time, secular and ecclesial organizations strive to bring about justice for whales, for forests, for battered wives and abused children, for the poor, for victims of oppression—all these causes are worthy. Yet most of these efforts have remained fragmented, isolated from each other.

Liberation theology, with its preferential option for the poor, has helped us to recognize the poor and the oppressed as a primary source of divine presence. Similarly, through integral ecology, we begin to see in our present moment of cultural collapse and ecological devastation, the Earth itself as a source of divine wisdom. In the words of Thomas Berry, "If there is no spirituality in the Earth, then there is no spirituality in ourselves. The human and the Earth are totally implicated each in the other." This communion summons us to engagement, and challenges us to embrace the fragile planet that brings us not only sunflowers and moonlight but also hurricanes and AIDS and spina bifida.

Justice for the Earth is a work of the heart—a falling in love with the divine voice that summons us to become one with the beautiful and oppressed Earth. Geo-justice is more a means for participation than an obligation—more about love than about laws, more about harmony than have-tos. Geo-justice extends the compassion of the heart into the psyche, society, and Earth. It is about healing ourselves, our systems, and our planet.

Myths bring energy to people, shaping their perceptions, unifying their vision. To undo our present ecological devastation, we need a new myth. Geo-justice is an operative myth for our time.

Geo-justice is a preferential option promising justice for the whole Earth and its people. In this perspective, no significant decision or action occurs without assessing how that action or decision would affect the Earth.

As we move toward this preferential option, we can draw

upon the theological paradigms from the past and rediscover and reinvigorate their meaning. When I review my own personal journey and the ways in which I explored social and ecological justice through my own writing, I find two complementary paradigms that, taken together, offer tremendous potential for understanding our way forward. These paradigms are the trinitarian perspective and the Paschal mystery.

In this chapter, I discuss each of these paradigms and the relevance it holds for us now. The following section in the book expands on the trinitarian perspective, with a chapter devoted to each of its three dynamic principles. The sections that follow that expand on the elements of the Paschal mystery.

A Trinitarian Perspective

When I first was introduced to Thomas Berry's creation spirituality and the new cosmology, I was confronted with a challenging question: how could I integrate my background in community development and organization with what I was learning about the universe and the three dynamic principles named by Teilhard de Chardin and Thomas Berry? These three principles are *differentiation* (nothing in the universe is the same), *communion* (everything in the universe is interconnected and interdependent), and *interiority* (there is deep subjectivity, consciousness, in each expression of creation).

I coined the term geo-justice to represent the incorporation of my past experience into what I was discovering about spirituality and cosmology. Specifically, differentiation became the context for justice in the local here-and-now of our lives; communion became the global dimension of our planetary reality; and interiority became the psycho-social component.

The theological expression of the trinity is the Father,

Son, and Holy Spirit. When we reflect on geo-justice from a trinitarian perspective, we see that differentiation is the expression of the creator God (Father); interiority is the expression of the word (Son) that is the source of the story; and communion is the expression of cosmic connection and interdependence (Holy Spirit). When these three components become manifest in cultural form, the divine is palpable and present in our midst. Here, the work of geo-justice becomes both a source of justice and an instrument to resacralize the Earth.

I went on to further develop the geo-justice vision and ground it in additional components of dialogue and theology. I called this further development *engaged cosmology*, borrowing from the term *engaged Buddhism*, used by monk Thích Nhat Hanh; the vision of liberation theology, as originally expressed by Gustavo Gutiérrez; and the Catholic Action method of "see, judge, and act."

Our work in geo-justice is founded on the conviction that our lives are governed and guided by three principles that provide a focus for how to live. In a very clear way, we can say that the universe is coded to provide guidance for what enhances life on Earth. Each of us who is privileged to live at this time in history is challenged to discover our true destiny, identity, and purpose, which together give voice to who we are and why we are here.

Differentiation refers to the uniqueness woven into the universe. Every snowflake, every person, is different. To comprehend each rock, flower, bird, or human is to see how it is different from the others. The cultural metaphor of the melting pot does not fit here; the image of a mosaic is much more appropriate. Each is different from the other, a particular experience of beauty. Everything has something to give that nothing else can give. Each creature is a unique manifestation of the divine, with a special gift and responsibility.

You experience differentiation in your life when you write a poem that no one has yet expressed. You experience it when you form unique friendships with each person you know. You experience it when you appreciate each tree in the forest as a unique sacred presence.

Through differentiation, we are each faced with the challenge to be uniquely who we are, because we are distinct from any other person on Earth. To be uniquely ourselves requires that we not base our identity on any other or imitate anyone else. In addition, to discover our own destiny and purpose requires that what we have to give to the world can only be given by us.

Interiority means that the universe is made up of subjects, each possessing a capacity for deep interior experience. This interior experience releases energy to organize and sustain patterns of relationship in a specific way. Interiority refers to the configuration of the Milky Way, to the way geese fly in formation, and to human interaction manifest in the self or a cultural form such as education or government. Everything carries within it the deep mystery of its capacity for existence and experience of the divine.

You experience interiority when you spend a quiet evening reading and reflecting on a book. You experience it as you take in the beauty of a sunset. You experience it in the silence of a forest.

Through interiority, we are challenged to activate a new religious sensitivity that opens us to the wonder and awe of the universe that we become conscious of at the floorboards of our souls. From this place we recognize and express our inner voice. Our culture needs to find its voice and listen with a deep sensitivity to the voices of each member of the Earth community. Only when we awaken to listen to the brook, the bird, and the migrant in the barrio will we cease to plunder and destroy.

Communion implies relationship. Communion teaches us that seemingly discrete entities are also interconnected and bonded into a pattern of togetherness with all that is. Similarly, communion culturally extends to us the opportunity to belong, while differentiation challenges us to retain our own uniqueness. We are bonded into a pattern of togetherness with all that is.

You experience communion when you appreciate that you are not alone on this planet, that you are connected with all of humanity. You experience it when you participate with neighbors to insist that your community have a clean source of drinking water.

Through communion, we celebrate interdependence and the realization that relationship is in fact the foundation of existence. Deep relationships heal alienation and separation. We have a capacity for relationship, a gravitational attraction that must extend from ourselves to other humans, to the natural world, to all that is. Only so will life on this planet survive, flourish, and be permeated with compassion.

Geo-justice provides an opportunity to explore what we observe in the world through the eyes of science and of the Christian gospel. This reflection can lead to actions through which we are able to heal the discrepancy between our vision and our practice, to heal the divide between the world as it is and the world as we would like it to be, between the personal, social, and ecological.

Pope Francis writes, "We are part of nature.... It is essential to seek comprehensive solutions which consider the interactions within natural systems themselves and with social systems.... Strategies for a solution demand an integrated approach to combating poverty, restoring dignity to the excluded, and at the same time protecting nature."

The tenets of integral ecology broadcast in the writings of Leonardo Boff and Thomas Berry have now been powerfully and urgently announced to the world by the pastor of the planet, Pope Francis. We have reason to hope and anticipate a time when the poor can be fed and housed and the natural world restored and celebrated. I envision a time when we no longer need to worry that our children and our children's children will be living in Rachel Carson's "silent spring." Instead, it will be a new time of conversion at every level, a time of spiritual, theological, structural, and organizational reconstruction. A new world will become possible, a world that is inclusive, interdependent, and interrelated.

The Paschal Mystery Reimagined

Many years ago I became gripped with a desire to understand change, its meaning, and implication for our lives. Initially, I saw change as the transition from one state to another. Later, I came to see that transition is best expressed as an act of transformation. I understand transformation as an event whereby something ceases to exist and something new is born.

From a theological perspective, our journey begins with a here-and-now event, an event that represents birth (incarnation). In the process, that event ceases to exist (death). And out of this dying event something new comes into existence; out of nothingness, newness is born (resurrection).

I understand that this process encompasses all events where transformation happens in our lives. We witness the rhythm of each day as it progresses through light, darkness, and light again. Today when the sun came up in the East, a new day was born; this represents incarnation. This evening when the sun sets in the West, darkness will descend upon the land; this represents crucifixion. Tomorrow at the break of dawn, the night will be dispelled, as we rise to another day; this is the resurrection moment of Easter. At this moment, we die to ourselves and rise to a concern for others.

Similarly, each year we flow through the seasons of spring, summer, fall, and winter. Our lives are marked by birth, life, death, and rebirth. These events are dynamic, mysterious, and woven into the very fabric of existence.

A transformation is taking place both in our culture and in our consciousness. Old forms and paradigms are collapsing. We live at the moment of both breakdown and breakthrough. The breakdown invites us to be hospice workers; the breakthrough, to be midwives. By creating a hospice for the culture, a context in which old cultural forms can die with dignity, we make it possible for new forms to be born.

Chaplains who do hospice work often ask their patients, "How has cancer blessed your life?" I have met people recovering from heart attacks who told me the illness had created a new beginning in their lives. From apparent tragedy emerges the beginning of a new perspective on life.

Our challenge as workers in geo-justice is to see how the cancer and heart attacks of the Earth are signs of resurrection and not just of death. Theologically, they are an intense and critical enactment of the Paschal mystery in our midst.

We will only achieve a new understanding by immersing ourselves in these crises of the world, not by escaping from them. Geo-justice calls us to immerse ourselves in the fabric of life. History teaches us that engagement in life is a prerequisite for cultural transformation.

The dynamics of breakdown and breakthrough at the societal level reflect the individual's experience of transition. Change, for a society or an individual, begins with a sense of disquiet, a recognition that all is not as it should be, and that events are moving us in the wrong direction. Neither an individual nor a culture should stay stuck in personal or social malaise.

In the face of uncertainty and widespread fear at levels not experienced in recent decades, we stand poised at a moment of transition, a moment of letting go of the past and awaiting something new to emerge. Like acrobats on a trapeze, we have to let go of one rope before we can grab for the next. We don't know what will come. But we are confident that something good will come forth.

As midwives for a new ecological era and hospice workers for a culture about to die, we need to address two important questions:

What needs to be born?
What needs to die?

Within the Paschal mystery, dying is a transformative act that is recycled into new life. The Paschal mystery of the incarnation, crucifixion, resurrection, and Pentecost is the story of every Christian, and also the story of the Earth.

The resurrection is both the centerpiece of the Christian story and its most amazing aspect. Resurrection implies the revitalization of our lives and of the Earth. It is the deepest act of transformation possible, whereby something dies and subsequently comes back to life transformed.

With eyes of faith, we are able to see resurrection

everywhere: in the seed that dies into the dark earth only to rise as a vital flowering plant, in the caterpillar that loses its identity in the stage of the chrysalis only to rise again as a beautiful butterfly. Each can be seen as a symbol of resurrection, a sign of vitality and new life arising out of death.

The sending of the Spirit, the Pentecost moment, is a central act of the risen Christ. The sending of the Spirit happens when we have the courage to come together as a community. Separations are bridged, alienations healed. It is as if we are no longer alone. We remember the promise of the post Resurrection—that the risen Christ will not abandon us. He will send the Spirit to encourage us to heal what separates us. He will send the Spirit to bind up the wounds of separation and loneliness.

Through the Paschal mystery, death and new life are woven together into a tapestry of ecological health and social justice. Geo-justice becomes an operative vision for creating harmony and balance on the Earth, in our community, and within ourselves.

The Paschal mystery story culminates in the Pentecost event. Pentecost unites what had been separated; it offers healing and the promise of community. In geo-justice, a planetary Pentecost calls forth the birth of a new Earth, a new people, a new creation.

Through the lens of geo-justice, we view the events of our planet as a reenactment of the Paschal mystery. We move from cherishing the pristine beauty of the Earth to enduring the cosmic crucifixion of ecological devastation and social injustice; we move to viewing the empty tomb, from which finally the hope arises of new life in a Pentecost for the planet.

We are invited in this moment to become instruments of geo-justice and architects of a planetary Pentecost. I am convinced that the path to a planetary Pentecost calls for a convergence of our collective energies. This invitation is as strong as a gravitational pull. I call it a *magnetic intuition*. It calls forth that which is deepest, most fascinating, and most wonderful to us, and invites us to respond.

Central to the challenge of embracing the Paschal mystery in our lives is the practice of letting go. I think that the dual efforts of letting go and letting be are the most significant practices of the spiritual journey.

The letting go process involves transition from life, to death, to new life. We are challenged to die daily and rise to a concern for others. Most profoundly, at the end of our mortal lives, we surrender to our physical death. We surrender into the arms of an all-loving God and are mysteriously embraced by the surprise of new life.

As Pope Francis writes about integral ecology and challenges us to heal the Earth and care for the poor, his words take on a Paschal mystery meaning. He invites us to enter courageously into a new resurrection moment for the Earth and its people. This will be a time when the air is clear, the water pure, and the land fertile once again. It will be an Easter moment in which the poor of the world are healed of their hunger and are able to live joyfully, and to bring enthusiasm to their days and beauty to the world.

Process Reflection: Learning from the Prophets

The world has known many prophets who have offered their wisdom across the centuries. When I teach or write, I like to incorporate wise words from more than a single tradition to reflect the diversity of our human perspective. This exercise can be done alone or in a group.

1. Set up a mood that invites a felt connection to God: slides, music, related readings from the mystics. Take time for silence and meditation.
2. Each participant names one widely known prophet who has influenced his or her life. As a group, compare how these messages are similar or different. If you are doing this alone, name three prophets and compare them.
3. Each participant reflects on his or her own mystical experiences, those transcendent moments when one is aware of being a part of something much larger than oneself. In a group, summarize the common themes emerging from discussion and responses; if alone, put your reflections into your journal.

Process Reflection: Wisdom Circle

This process is designed to assist a group to both listen to each other and share their feelings and insights in response to an identified geo-justice issue with current relevance to the community.

1. Begin the process with music and/or a brief ritual.
2. Sit in a circle.
3. The leader selects an artifact as the "talking stick."
4. The leader poses a question that speaks to the participants.
5. A member who wishes to respond, asks for the talking stick. The others refrain from any cross talk as they listen to the person speaking.
6. When everyone has spoken, the leader closes the circle with a brief ritual.

What Do You Hear?

When I deeply listen to earth,
something sacred happens.
Stories of beauty and brokenness are told.
Grandmother tree tells of her grief,
about how her leaves and branches
were all torn and tossed about.

Listen, listen, over there.
Hear the prayer lodge speak
from the place where sacred salutations
are offered to the Holy One on high.

Listen, listen, to your companions:
water in the swamp,
crow in the sky,
fawn in the field.
Shelly the dog stands guard
at the big house, by the door.
Oak saplings tell of their terror in the storm.

Listen, listen, do you hear what I hear?
Our companions of creation
proclaim their great "I am's":
I am thunder. I am rain.
I am Matthew. I am pain.
I am sunrise. I am dusk.

I am beauty. I am broken.
I am ancient. I am new.
I am silence. I am song.
I am Earth. And so are you.

Chapter 3
Toward an Operative Theology of Geo-Justice

In the present condition of global society, where injustices abound and growing numbers of people are deprived of basic human rights and considered expendable, the principle of the common good immediately becomes, logically and inevitably, a summons to solidarity and a preferential option for the poorest of our brothers and sisters.
> **—Pope Francis** (*Laudato Si'*, 158)

The process whereby we integrate our actions with what we know to be true is theological reflection. When our actions flow from what we know is true, we call it operative theology.

We are being called today to develop an operative theology—a gospel of the moment—that can respond to the following question: What are the deepest convictions that guide my life and that have their roots in my tradition?

I invite people to connect what they intuitively understand to be right and just with what they see embodied in their Christian tradition. This, in turn, sheds new light on their engagement in the world.

An example of operative theology can be found in the response of the Dene people of Canada's Northwest Territories to a question posed by Remi Fumoleau, OMI, after he had taught them all he had learned in his theological studies. He asked, "What of all that I have taught you do you consider the most important aspect of the Christian faith?"

The answer came back: "Never lock your door."

The operative theology of the Dene people was hospitality. For them, the most important way they could express their faith was to offer an opportunity to get out of the cold on a winter night.

Similarly, we are invited to make connections between our deepest convictions and a gospel view that sheds light on those convictions. When we experience congruence between our visceral convictions and our Christian faith, something remarkable happens. We experience fresh energy that activates our imagination and prompts us to be liberated from imposed patterns of living and acting.

We should not expect this movement toward a new theology to be worked out in advance. This theology will evolve through a process of reflection and action. We admire the beauty of the Earth; we listen to its pain; we act out our preferential option for the Earth; we reflect on the state of our planet, in light of what we most deeply trust is true. Thus we develop a theology of geo-justice.

A Drink from Our Own Well: The Process of Theological Reflection

Through the process of theological reflection, geo-justice makes us increasingly aware of the connection between our actions and what we believe in most deeply. Theological reflection releases enormous energy. By learning to listen to our inner promptings, we recognize God's creative energy as the source of personal and social transformation.

Theological reflection sheds new light on how to integrate the vision of the world we aspire to create and the gospel that guides our lives.

Theological reflection can occur within us individually or within groups. We explore how questions of identity, justice, and self-determination can be understood as congruent with the gospel, whereby each of us discovers ourselves as the creative subject of our own future. In a collective conversation, each member becomes both teacher and student. We learn from each other.

Theological reflection, in the context of geo-justice, explores the congruence between our mystical, prophetic, and personal experiences and our global awareness, local action, and societal vision. Theological reflection in geo-justice opens us to an operative theology of the Earth, a gospel view that sees the Earth as the poor, the voiceless, and the locus of divine action. Gustavo Gutierrez, the liberation theologian from Peru, asserts in *We Drink From Our Own Wells* that theological reflection builds on commitment and faith.

Theological reflection challenges us to trust our imagination as we apply our deepest experiences of awe, protest, and self-discovery to the concrete circumstances of our lives. It integrates what we most deeply trust with how we act. Theological reflection aligns faith and life; it brings to the surface an intuitive value system that gives meaning and purpose to our lives.

The practice of theological reflection in geo-justice ensures that the actions that flow from our reflection will be responsive to the needs of the Earth. This reflection has three steps.

- We examine our deepest convictions, revealed in mysticism, prophecy, and personal experience.
- We seek congruence between these convictions and our view of the Earth as the locus of the divine.
- We develop transformative actions to heal the Earth.

Such an approach to theological reflection is responsive both to our own experience and to the needs of the Earth. It sheds new light on our traditions and encourages us to discover possibilities for action in every area of our lives. It prevents us from uncritically accepting imposed patterns of living and acting.

From this experience of trusting the Earth and ourselves, a new language is born, new realizations awakened. We are empowered by the intentions of the Earth itself, and we become instruments of healing.

We live in a time when world trade, global communication, economic practices, science, technology, commerce, and domestic life are all undergoing profound changes. This period has two characteristics: old ways of organizing experience no longer serve as accurate descriptions of the way things are, and new ways of organizing experience can be confusing until a new worldview crystallizes. We know that old structures are breaking down, but we do not yet see clearly the form of the new structures and possibilities.

The Cosmic Christ

When I initially began to frame the theology of geo-justice, I became convinced that an adequate theology needs to be based in an evolutionary perspective. That alone makes it possible to heal the inherent dualism in the Christian tradition that separates God from the world.

Teilhard de Chardin gave us a vision of the Cosmic Christ that is based on an understanding of evolution. In light of his vision, contemporary views of an unfolding universe are congruent with the Christian perspective, as revealed in sacred scripture and found in the New Testament (especially, the Gospel of John and the Pauline Letters).

Teilhard saw Christ as a cosmic one who is immense,

present, and universal—a resurrected Christ who is as vast as the world, who is "the soul of the world" and an organic center of the universe. Teilhard said, "To live the cosmic life is to live dominated by the consciousness that one is an atom in the body of the mystical and Cosmic Christ." This Cosmic Christ began at the fireball that marked the turbulent origin of the universe and continues today as a universal, ongoing process. In this process, we have a fusion of scientific knowledge and divine wisdom.

Through our scientific understanding of evolution, we are able to experience a mystical vision of the world that is alive and unfolding. We perceive God at the center of this evolutionary process. It is a process whereby each member of creation bears the imprint of divinity and is centered on a vision of the Cosmic Christ.

In a very real way, we have to discover the universe before we can behold a universal Christ. And when we do the latter, we can recover a sense of the whole that is focused on Christ. Meister Eckhart wrote that "every creature is a book about God." St. Paul spoke of the divine intent "to unite all things in Christ, things in heaven and things on earth." Thus we see that the image of God is present in all things.

The Cosmic Christ can be understood as a pattern that connects. This pattern represents a synthesis of Christ and the universe, a mystery interpreted in light of modern science, and understood as an unfinished and developmental process that takes on its full value when extended to the cosmic dimension. This is not so much a Christ who rules, but rather a Christ who infuses divine creative energy into the world.

Teilhard's notion of the Cosmic Christ is deeply incarnational. He saw all matter as infused with the divine, and he considered all of creation as "the body and blood" of the Christ. His is a vision of faith grounded in the bible, yet infused with the evolutionary focus of the modern world.

This view has not dominated throughout the ages. For example, during the Black Death in the fourteenth century, due to their limited knowledge of disease, people concluded that God was angry with the world. As a result, they sought salvation through escape from the world. The Cosmic Christ was diminished in people's minds. Two centuries later, Newton and other scientists of the day explained the world solely through the language of mind and machine.

When we view the world through awakened evolutionary eyes, we see that it had a Christ dimension from the beginning. Through John's gospel, which says, "In the beginning was the word," we realize that the world was created in and through God Himself. The journey of Christ can be seen as progressing from the preexistent word to the incarnate word and then to the transfigured word. The Cosmic Christ encompasses all three of these phases. As we reinterpret Christianity through a new consciousness, we shift from an emphasis on the historical Jesus to an emphasis on the Cosmic Christ.

A New Era of Christianity

The Cosmic Christ represents a new theological orientation, a neo-Christianity. This new era of Christianity will save Christ from the hands of those who would deaden Him with outmoded rites and static dogma. It will revitalize our spirituality. It will heal the distance between Christianity and the modern world by reflecting on the cosmic nature of the mystery of Christ and its significance for our world today.

In a Cosmic Christ theology, we come to believe that the Christian story is identical with the universe story. We are united in a call to wholeness, to a relationship with the Cosmic Christ wherein life is viewed as a dynamic energy full of promise, vibrancy, and potential. With this in mind, the dualism that separates Christians from the world can be healed and people empowered to deal with social and ecological injustice.

As we move forward, we are awakening to the emergence of the Cosmic Christ being reborn again and again within and among us. With Teilhard, we affirm and celebrate that within the heart of matter is the heart of God.

It is only in and through this rebirth of oneness, manifest in the reunion of heaven and Earth, that the Christian journey can be revived. This embrace of oneness makes possible a rebirth of our relationship with the divine and the sacredness of all creation. This cosmic perspective also links Christianity with other world religions. When we affirm that consciousness was present from the beginning of the universe, regardless of what name we give it, we can understand it as coming from a common source. There is not just a Christian well or a Jewish mountain or a Buddhist tree, but there is a uniting, ecumenical vision that transcends these traditions that are perceived as separate.

Teilhard spoke about the unification of consciousness as the Omega Point. He explained the sequence of transformational events leading up to this point as a movement that spans the domains of physics, geology, biology, anthropology, and other sciences, and that takes us from the formation of the universe, through the development of human culture, and ultimately to the divine. Life is thus drawn toward the Omega Point, the yet-to-be-fulfilled future reality that is not fixed but always evolving. Teilhard foresaw a new global stage of consciousness and technology that made possible a noosphere—a world mind that is increasingly unified.

Citizens of the Cosmos

The natural world, which we can understand as the divine dream of Creation, has woven into its very fabric an opaque dimension. The Earth community has both a peaceful and a violent expression. This apparent polarity was present at the great flaring forth and is still present today.

Consider the original super nova event. Through an enormous explosion, the elements were formed. It was both a violent and a powerfully creative moment that prepared the way for our planet's birth and for human life.

Suppose you have two balls of clay; one is black and the other is white. We could say for the sake of this example that the black represents what is good and the white represents what is evil. If you take the two balls and kneed them into a single ball, the result is a grey sphere of clay. In the same way, within creation, all pairs of opposites—transparent and opaque, good and evil, hot and cold, large and small, and so on—are woven into one integrated whole. This whole is the sum total of the divine energy of the universe.

Geo-justice invites us to become open to the divine creative energy of the universe, as it manifests in our life and work. We have an experience of being drawn by powerful yet open-ended forces. The irresistibility of this invitation is a sign of the power of these forces within us. They push us to risk moving beyond however we may have defined the contours of our life's work, toward an experience that is indefinable but inevitable, consistent but constantly changing, always unfinished but complete in itself.

Access to this fuller and deeper way of living is nourished and focused by moments of reflection and solitude. Often these moments provide the opportunity to respond to an invitation of some other—be it a person, an idea, a plant, or an animal. The propensity to fall in love, to expand our horizons, to achieve a sense of wholeness—all these increase our awareness.

We become acutely aware of the inherent dialectic in interdependence. The moment-by-moment choices we make preclude any sets of presuppositions and guidelines. We are on our own. At the same time, we are supported by the emerging consensus of an expanding global community. We are independent and autonomous, yet we are interdependent and part of a vast movement taking place around the world. Our awareness of this dialectic generates solidarity and purpose, dissolves despair, and supports courage in listening to our inner voice as we pursue unpredictable paths.

Knowing our place in the cosmos is a lifelong and continuous process. It deepens, expands, and is constantly accompanied by unknowing and uncertainty. In accessing the unknown, we search for a more profound source from which to live.

At the same time, the energy of the cosmos provides opportunity to awaken to the deep significance of our own journeys. Our interest and passion are as fragile as our endangered planet. Yet like butterflies flashing with color in an afternoon garden, each one matters and contributes to the beauty of the whole.

In this journey of faith, we discover the palpable presence of the divine. A growing global awareness anchors us in the cosmos. The divine presence awakens primordial energies in our bodies, and we feel ourselves connected with all of creation. Our prophetic contribution to the universe captivates and enchants us. Cosmic wisdom unfolds life's surprises. Our privilege is to be open to the moment of the unexpected.

Process Reflection: The Four Creatures

We tend to be human-centric creatures. This may be especially true for those who spend all their time in urban areas. Geo-justice calls on us to be citizens of the cosmos, and that includes appreciating and empathizing with all forms of life. Have fun with this exercise: it can be done alone or in a group.

1. Identify with one of the following four types of creatures
    Winged (air)
    *   Fish (water)
    *   Four-legged (earth)
    *   Mythological (e.g., dragon) (fire)
2. Write a poem or prose poem about your chosen creature. It might depict your unique relationship with the universe or with the planet. Or it might be a metaphor for how you move through the world.
3. If you are in a group, come together to share your poems. If you are doing this on your own, you might email your poem to a friend or share it on social media.
4. Generate a list of actions you can take in light of your reflections on the various types of creatures.
    *   Actions related to winged creatures might focus on air pollution
    *   Actions related to fish might focus on cleaning up the oceans
    *   Actions related to four-legged creatures might focus on animal rights.
    *   Actions related to mythological creatures might focus on power relationships

Process Reflection: Outline for Theological Reflection

In this chapter, I listed what I see as the three phases of theological reflection in geo-justice (examining our convictions, seeking congruence, and taking transformative action). This exercise provides a way to follow this process in a group.

1. Share the following (phase of examining our convictions):
   - Who you are and your pressing global, local, and personal concerns
   - What you perceive the problems to be
   - What you have done about these problems up till now
   - What is needed to resolve the problems/concerns perceived
2. Discuss (phase of seeking congruence):
   - What themes emerged from the four questions covered in the biographical and descriptive phase?
3. Use the themes as a lens to develop a deeper and more comprehensive understanding of the issues (phase of transformative actions):
   - Personal experience: What do you see that relates to your life? How does it make you feel?
   - Group experience: What similarities in personal experiences can be recognized by the group?
   - Larger context: What is the larger picture that your experience is part of?
   - Action: What are appropriate actions to take from the perspective of geo-justice?
   - Critique: How are our proposed actions congruent with or contradictory to our faith perspective?

Tell Me a Story

Tell me a story
about the land where you were born,
the land of your ancestors,
where sacred tales are told.

Speak to me
about the beauty of this place,
about the wonder of waterfalls and trees.
Please tell me
about mountain tops, valleys and streams,
crops in the fields.
About companions on the land,
and joy in your heart.

Speak about your memories
of the deep blue sky
and stars that twinkle in the night.
Tell me about your ancestors,
the first people who settled
in this sacred place
you call home.

Tell the story of the plant people
who made this land their home
and nourished your ancestors
so long ago.
And speak about the sacred waters
that irrigate your homeland
and whet your soul.

Yes, tell me
about your cousins of creation,
both great and small,
who made this land their home.
About birds in the sky,
horses on the hill,
fish in the river.

Tell the stories you heard as a child,
about your first communion,
when the Ancient One of ancient days
revealed herself to you,
that ever-precious moment
when you shivered with delight
and knew what you had to do,
and began.

Tell stories of dreams
that lay bare the glory of a new day
and the courage to engage
with the challenges of life,
big, wondrous dreams of generosity and service
that you will share with others,
as your hearts fill with wonder
at the stories of a tomorrow yet untold.

PART II:
Three Dynamic Principles

Chapter 4
The Components of Geo-Justice

Peace is built day by day …. It is not an industrial product, it is an artisanal product. It is crafted every day with our work, with our life, with our closeness.
> **—Pope Francis** (May 11, 2015, at the Vatican's Peace Factory)

The work of geo-justice is predicated on the conviction that to get our lives in order within society and the soul, we must be in alignment with the empirical observation of the three dynamic principles of the universe. In other words, any true understanding of the divine must be congruent with the understanding of the universe we gain from science.

The dynamic principles of the universe, as described in chapter two, are the trinitarian principles of differentiation, interiority, and communion.

When our life moves according to these principles, we begin to approach our dream of a new culture and restored Earth. A culture developed in this way will deepen our experience of wisdom and mystery. When communion, differentiation, and interiority are present, not only is the culture reborn, but the divine is palpable and present in trinitarian form. We can assert that the rebirth of culture is more about relationship than rules, more about connectedness than accomplishment. It is both fluid and fixed, a quilted tapestry that is both distinct and one.

The Dynamic Principles and Their Associated Components

Looking at these three dynamic principles from a different perspective, we see that they are developed through three components: local, psychosocial, and global. They are like identifiable parts of the "stew" that is geo-justice. They interact with and influence each other.

- The here-and-now local level is where the cosmic principle of differentiation takes place. This local level can be understood as a bioregion—a location on the Earth where the rocks, waters, trees, and land form a functional community that supports both the people and the planet. Differentiation finds its expression at the local level through our expressions of uniqueness and creativity. For example, if we bemoan the problems of a failing infrastructure in an overly general manner, change is unlikely to follow. However, if we can focus on a particular local context, we have a place to begin. By becoming aware of the toxic levels of lead in their water, the community of Flint, Michigan, can take action to clean up their water. And by becoming aware of their efforts, you can follow suit and learn about the level of lead or other chemicals in your own community, and take action, as well.

- The psychosocial component emerges out of the cosmic principle of interiority. It points to the need for congruence between our interior life (psyche) and our actions in the world (social). Our actions must be not only congruent with our beliefs, but they must also be aligned with our commitment to justice. For example, this alignment was lacking in those political officials who used toxic water in an attempt to save money at the expense of the health and well-being of children in Flint.

- The global component invites us to experience the Earth as a whole. Astronauts, such as Scott Kelly, who spent 340 days in space, are able to view our planetary home without the national boundaries we impose. The cosmic principle of communion opens us to the interconnectedness of all things. Experiencing the universe as one enhances the meaning of global solidarity. On the global level, we focus on our commonalities. We rely on trust and communication. Above all, we hold humanity and the Earth in an embrace of compassion.

In this dynamic system, components overlap: the global with the local, the local with the psycho-social. Looking at any one component is like using a zoom lens on a camera: we focus on one element of the whole picture, always remembering that it remains part of a larger unity. As we focus on one component, we need to keep in mind its interconnection with the other components. The global, local, and psycho-social intersect and interact; a change in any one has implications for the whole system.

The Micro and the Macro

There are two kinds of analysis: macro and micro. Micro-analysis puts things under a microscope—we attempt to understand them by examining in great detail some minute component of the whole. Macro-analysis refers to a study of the forces at play on a larger scale.

Weather patterns make a good example. Micro-analysis might study the effect of Lake Michigan on winter temperatures in Chicago; macro-analysis might try to understand that same Chicago winter weather by integrating the effects of ozone layer depletion, the position and strength of the jet stream, and ocean currents in the South Pacific.

Many groups today deal with justice issues from a local perspective, while others engage in their work from a global perspective. What seems frequently missing is an understanding of the micro/macro interrelationship, whereby everything is related to everything else. Any part potentially contains within itself the whole, and the whole affects every part.

By developing a local/global imagination, we can hold in dynamic tension the part and the whole, the micro and the macro, the prophetic and the mystical, the local and the global, the past and the future. We examine the social movements of the past and present to nourish our imaginations and to critique present actions. The agrarian protest of the nineteenth century, the labor struggle of the 1920s, the Black power movement of the 1950s and 1960s, the work of community organization and the environmental movement that continue to today—all give us insights into present justice work. They also give us courage to carry on.

Experience and history teach us that the justice makers have always been a minority. Yet that minority provides hope and inspiration for many. Our hope for geo-justice is to broaden that minority. We need more people engaged in long-term efforts to liberate the structures and emotions that hold us back.

This process is not evaluated in terms of winning or losing. We view it instead from a perspective that sees the struggle itself as victory, and success as a commitment to a different worldview. The only failure is the failure to be hopeful, to be involved, and to learn from our experiences.

The local approach weaves together a tapestry of action and numinous mystery. Each thread affects the whole tapestry. Each part, each action, has its own integrity. It is alive. Each action can continue to influence events. And it is mysterious, for it engages us at a very deep level.

As we develop the mystical consciousness and global analysis dimensions of geo-justice, we discover that the process of justice making for the whole Earth cries out for a local perspective. Albert Nolan, in *God in South Africa*, writes, "The paradigm that shapes every prophetic movement, no matter what its context, is simply this—the time has come, the day is near." That urgency, that imperative to do something, certainly characterizes our time.

Igniting the imagination for geo-justice involves putting forth narratives wherein the drama of people's lives can unfold. Hope comes alive through new images and new perspectives that emerge from the people's lived experiences. From this approach to creativity comes the focused energy necessary to transform a culture. Only then can we empower the building of civil and economic alternatives for the future.

Process Reflection: The Three Principles

Although I included examples to show how the three principles of the universe manifest at the local, psycho-social, and global levels, these ideas can sound quite abstract. For this reason, it is important to examine these principles and see how they translate into cultural form to embody the work of geo-justice and ecological integration. This exercise can be done alone or in a group.

1. How would you describe the three principles of the universe? Do you agree there are three?
2. How can these principles provide a compass for our work of cultural renewal?
3. Can you imagine ways that differentiation fosters acts of creativity at the local level in your life?
4. Besides interiority, what other forces can lead us to be more sensitive to the sacredness of all creatures?
5. Besides communion, what other forces encourage others to reach out with compassion to the needy?

Process Reflection: The Sacred Waters of Our Common Story

Water can be a powerful symbol for the sacred. Water is a sacrament as well as the most essential element for life to exist on our planet. This exercise is done in a group.

1. Play music, such as Hildegard von Bingen's "A Feather on the Breath of God."
2. Invite each participant to bring to the circle a sample of water from his or her home. If this is not convenient, give each person a paper cup of water and have each speak of the water as coming from the ocean, river, lake, or pond where he or she lived as a child.
3. Place a glass bowl on a stand in the center of the room.
4. Participants come forward one by one and speak to the group about the "sacred water of my childhood."

5. The process is closed by the passing of a talking stick around the circle, and the group reflects on how this ritual has created a metaphor for community.

All I Have to Say

I want to tell you about the world
we hope to live in.

A world that's welcoming,
where we all belong.

Not a world that is static and stuck,
full of abstractions and ideas;
rather a world of compassion and love.

A place of belonging and hope,
where every puppy, plant and person
awakens each morning to a wondrous day.

A world full of enthusiasm and zest.
This is all I have to say.

Chapter 5

Uniqueness and Creativity: The Local Component

Life is an adventure of passion, risk, danger, laughter, beauty, love, a burning curiosity to go with the action to see what it is all about, to search for a pattern of meaning, to burn one's bridges because you're never going to go back anyway.

—Saul Alinsky (*Reveille for Radicals*, p viii, 1946)

Creativity in the context of our local community flows from a deep appreciation and respect for diversity. One of the most pressing issues at the local level for us in the San Francisco Bay Area is the need for affordable housing. Each week, when I am in Berkeley, I travel to St. Mary's Center to participate in their housing clinic. In this program, whose motto is "Everyone needs a place," a group of displaced people gather weekly in search of an address they can call home. Many have lived in transitional housing, others in cardboard condos or storefronts or their cars for some time. Each week they fill out applications, make phone calls to investigate vacancies, and sign up to return the following week to continue the process. Even with the help they receive at St. Mary's, it takes most a long time to find a place to call home.

In this era, as the chasm between the affluent and the impoverished continues to grow, the challenges presented for displaced people are exceedingly high. The response demands creativity born out of an appreciation for diversity. In the case of St. Mary's, creativity means viewing each person as deserving, and responding out of an abiding sense of decency. It means looking beyond traditional options. It means not giving up.

At the same time, the creative process reveals more completely both our own individual uniqueness and our uniqueness as a community. It reveals the inherent beauty of that uniqueness. Creativity is about being drawn forward; allured; enchanted by a passion, a desire, and a fascination for beauty. Creativity is a spiritual response to each here-and-now situation. Our creativity may be expressed not in a painting or sculpture, but through the creative acts of raising a family, fashioning friendships, or offering support and solitude to those in need.

When a person is enchanted by the desire to play music, plant a garden, build an organization, or teach a class, surprises occur. Something erupts from the depths and everything shifts. There is an experience of being carried forward and embraced by the energy of the universe. This takes place in the context of a particular local community.

Creativity as an expression and path to uniqueness can also involve struggle. When I write, I struggle to put on paper what is on my mind and in my imagination. Part of my writing involves being vulnerable by revealing my thoughts and feelings to others. I have to struggle to escape from abstraction and become open to my own and other people's lived experience. Jean Shinoda Bolen describes creativity as similar to the attitude of a woman about to give birth: she unconditionally surrenders to whatever happens and to whoever shows up.

Another dimension of the creative process is that it is ongoing. I learned in community organization that one issue eventually leads to another, and another, and so on. A neighborhood project involving a parking problem leads to a landlord issue and then to a housing committee. Creativity involves being flexible enough to follow the dynamic as the process unfolds in a particular local context. The creative process is not linear or predictable, but rather full of surprises.

When we quit trying to control life and instead rise to its surprises, we are involved in creativity. Letting go is a difficult part of the process. A friend once told me about going to a seminar on using time. As she tells it, the central message of the several hours of class was that jotting down every activity, every moment of the day, every phone number, every interaction would somehow guarantee control of life. As the participants left the meeting, the leader asked my friend what she thought of the process. She responded that it had taken her fifty years to relinquish the illusion that she could control her life and she didn't intend to take it up again. She had realized over the years that harmony with the life forces around her was more important than ephemeral notions of control. She felt she was just beginning to live her life creatively.

Stifled Creativity

Creativity has not been espoused by bureaucratic institutions, nor has it been a central part of school curricula. In a financial crunch, it is the first thing to go. Creativity is, in fact, unwelcome in the structures of the dominant culture. Schools, corporations, and governments are interested in predictable behavior, not in the surging chaos of the unexpected. Doctors, lawyers, and clergy are schooled for uniformity. Each profession has a process of initiation that ensures predictable behavior and conformity.

It is common practice for large establishment organizations to violate uniqueness in the name of treating everyone equally. This rationale for sameness violates differences and promotes injustice. For example, the rich receive greater tax breaks than they otherwise might if they are placed in the same tax bracket as members of the middle class. Ethnic differences are blurred in the name of nationalism.

Pope Francis acknowledges the importance of celebrating differences. He emphasized this especially when speaking about refugees displaced from their homeland because of natural disasters or war, stating, "We must not be afraid of differences! Brotherhood allows us to discover that diversity is wealth, a gift for all."

The rebirth of culture we work for within our local communities must likewise celebrate differences. It must have a reverence for the differences of resources, ethos, language, and history. Much of the work performed in our culture is drenched in conformity, which promotes boredom and burnout. The people who perform these jobs year in and year out pay an enormous spiritual price. Creativity, meanwhile, can be an instrument for inspiration, joy, and healing. When a friend of mine began to write, she soon left her sick bed. In fact, she completed an entire manuscript in a few weeks. The powerful forces of creativity need to be channeled and not repressed. When this happens, healing can happen quickly.

In the creative process, we do not really know what to do next; we simply surrender any control and become astonished as we observe and celebrate what emerges. In this process of unleashing the wildness of our imagination into the culture, we celebrate rebirth and tap into a part of ourselves that remains untamed.

Creativity on the local level is a manifestation of our unique gifts and responsibility. Even while we may be working at the local level, we are simultaneously engaging in the evolutionary process of Earth; we are participating in the divine act of creating the cosmos. Each creative act is an epiphany that gives expression to unique microcosms that are our life. The adventure of creativity fashions our experience into tabernacles of mystery and depth. As a child brings home pictures from school to adorn the refrigerator door, we would do well to find expression in poetry, movement, and images for the ongoing creativity taking place in our souls. By honoring our imaginations and caring for our creativity, we engage in soul work and make our lives more meaningful and open to surprise.

Experiencing Creativity and Uniqueness

In each act of creativity, we are most fully human and most fully divine. Artists name their creative activity in intuitive language. Author D.H. Lawrence talks about "that spark that flies into consciousness… a little creative change." Artist Kenzi Myazawa writes, "We must forge our own beauty; we must set free the greyness of our labor with the art of our lives." Musician Miles Davis says, "I'll play it first and tell you about it later." Dancer Martha Graham, responding to an inquiry about her performance, comments, "I don't know. If I did, I wouldn't have done it." M. C. Richards, poet, painter, and potter, talks about her work this way: "The words bubble up and speak for themselves." Canadian artist Loren Harris states, "I strive to get to the summit of my soul and paint from there where the universe sings." Psychiatrist Stanislav Grof describes creativity as "agony and ecstasy and the fusion of both." Saul Alinsky, community organizer, acknowledges the need for creativity in cultural change: "The organizer is driven by a desire to create." And Brazilian educator Paulo Friere writes: "Education is an act of creation, unlocking other creative acts, a process from the inside out."

The creative process starts in the place we call home—in

school, in the workplace, in the street—and it extends to the far reaches of the Earth. Restoration of the Earth occurs first at the bioregional level, in the specific area of the Earth where we are awakening to our roots, both in nature and in culture. The opposite—environmental oppression—occurs when minority communities are chosen as toxic dumpsites, when suburbs spread unchecked over farmland, and when loggers clear-cut old-growth forests. These forms of oppression impose the needs and concerns of one community over those of another. Geo-justice brings a synthesis of socioeconomic concerns and ecological justice. We become present to the natural world in a respectful and non-evasive way, while at the same time seeing our oneness with nature as an indication of right relationships within society and with the planet.

The concrete action that identifies the local component of geo-justice is focused and energized by creation spirituality. The bioregion is the place to respond to the invitation "Bloom where you are planted." Thomas Berry defines a bioregion as a "self-propagating, self-nourishing, self-educating, self-governing, self-healing, and self-fulfilling community." Poet and essayist Gary Snyder writes, "Bioregional awareness teaches us in specific ways. It is not enough to just 'love nature' or to want to 'be in harmony with Gaia.' Our relation to the natural world takes place in a place, and it must be grounded in information and experience."

The Act of Justice Making

Organizing is the first act of justice making at the local level. It enables us to do together what we could not accomplish alone. Organizing is not so much about doing things for others as it is about creating the possibilities for people to do things for themselves. The classic example is that of either giving a hungry person a fish or organizing to provide a fishing pole so the hungry person has the means to obtain food.

When I studied community organization, I found that both the American community organizer Saul Alinsky and the Brazilian educator Paulo Freire articulated a four-phase approach to their work. The phases converge in unexpected ways. Their manner is different, but their intention is very much the same. I think it is helpful to examine their method as we develop the most effective process for our present cultural moment.

Phase I: Pre-organizing/Descriptive

This is the stage at which the organizer starts to work in the community. The intention is to build trust and listen to what the people have to say, without taking sides. The result of this process is to elevate the sense of hope and possibility among the people so they see themselves with increased dignity and value and begin to believe that they can accomplish something with their lives.

The initial phase is very much about dream and vision. Both Alinsky and Freire began with storytelling. They invited people to talk about their experiences and their hopes for a more just world. The initial storytelling provided the grounding. It assisted people in envisioning their world in a different way. People clarified their vision when they heard what others had to say. The story gathered energy and provided an opportunity to experience unity. For Alinsky, this was the *pre-organizing* phase. For Freire, it was the *descriptive* phase. In each case, people were invited to tell their stories and express their visions. This invariably generated a sense of hope. I was often told that "you organize with your ears." It is very true. In fact, Pope Francis echoes the importance of listening when he says, "Mostly, people are looking for someone to listen to them. Someone willing to grant them time, to listen to their dramas and difficulties. This is what I call the 'apostolate of the ear,' and it is important."

For Alinsky, organization provided the entry into people's greatest question: Why am I here? In light of this curiosity, which runs deep in all of us, he quoted scientist Niels Bohr: "Every sentence I utter must be understood not as an affirmation, but as a question." This essential attitude of curiosity is one of a cluster of characteristics that, when appropriately developed, constitute a radical commitment to change. The cluster also includes anger, imagination, sense of humor, discipline, singleness of purpose, native intelligence, and an organized personality. It is by integrating these characteristics that an organizer is most likely to find success.

Phase II: Disorganizing/Codification

The second phase focuses on the pain, obstacles, and structures that perpetuate injustice. For Alinsky, this was the *disorganizing* phase. It involved letting go of structures and dismantling systems that cause injustice. It involved shaking things up to form new patterns and relationships, new capacities to act.

For Freire, this second phase involved *codification*, or coding experience in a way that leads to naming the oppression. By this he meant identifying the internal obstacles and structural blocks that take away internal freedom and the capacity to make external choices. For the people of Brazil, the external block was the military regime; for us today, it may be financial and other institutional policies and the internal obstacle of fear.

The goal is to shake things up in the community. This is accomplished when patterns of power that exist at the service of the status quo are scrambled and disorganized in order to prepare for a new kind of structure that can be put to the service of people and the Earth.

In exploring the disorganizing phase, Alinsky uses the analogy of water. Just as hydrogen and oxygen need to let go of their identities to form water, so it is necessary that the diverse elements of a community be brought together so they can comprise an appropriate constellation for the new community organization.

The birth of a new organization is preceded by a letting go of old attitudes of heart and mind, as well as of the need for instant results. It also involves a willingness to step aside and allow people to take power. As organizers, we must be willing to let go of the resignation and fatalism that reside within each of us, and get in touch with the hope that burns deep within. We must be ready to let go of structure and predictability.

The continuing need for openness and flexibility on the part of organizers shows up when organizers see themselves as students as well as teachers. Organizers must be willing to change and be changed by the organizing process. In the phase of disorganization, they must set aside old ideas and be open to fresh solutions and creativity.

Years ago, I was a staff organizer with the Riverdale Community Organization. The first issue for discussion was that of absentee landlords, specifically the two owners of properties on Caroline Avenue. We began by taking the most obvious action: we invited them to our next meeting. Neither showed up.

We knew we had to do something differently. We had to be willing to embrace this state of disorganization, shake things up, and be more creative if we wanted to see change.

A dozen of us took it upon ourselves to travel to the distant upper-class neighborhood home of one landlady. It was a cold night, and we huddled outside while two went in to prepare the way. The rest soon followed, and the living room became our new forum.

The owner's excuses—such as "My husband is in the hospital"—were met by focusing on the bad conditions at the houses on Caroline Avenue. In this way, we named the situation. One member of our delegation said, "There have been three fires. You could be responsible for burning down our whole neighborhood."

The owner countered by asking, "How can you live in that area?"

We responded again by naming the issue: "What do you mean by 'that area'?"

The landlady pointed to one in our group: "You look like the smart one!" she said.

We had a response for that: "Are you saying the rest of us are stupid?"

The dialogue was heated, but it was also cordial. The landlady saw that we were serious about making change in the neighborhood. She gave us a verbal commitment to do some repairs. On the way home, we were so excited by the taste of victory that some wanted to go after the second landlord that night. We decided against it only because it was already 10:30 pm.

A letter was sent to the landlady to seal her commitment. Within a few days, the garages were repaired, and soon thereafter the interiors of the houses were improved.

Phase III: Organizing/Cultural Action

The third phase is about moving toward something new. For Alinsky, the *organizing* phase was about creating organizational forms for those who had no representation. He was fond of saying that "the organizer is driven by a desire to create." The organizer's work is to create organizations around issues for which there is no organizational response. For example, if a neighborhood has small children and working mothers, an organization to provide day care would be needed. Another need might be an afterschool program for children whose parents are still at work when they get out of school.

In probing the notion of creativity and breakthrough, Alinsky describes the organization as the vehicle of birth, and participation in it as the birth certificate for a new life. "The organization is born out of the issues and the issues are born out of the organization."

Freire also saw his work as a context for creativity. For him, education was the way we express creativity. The action that resulted was something we create. That something flowed from us, taught us, and ultimately transformed us. This was the phase of *cultural action*. He wrote, "Education is an act of creation, capable of unleashing other creative acts, a process from the inside out."

I can give you an example of the organizing phase from my time with the Riverdale Community Organization. One evening, as part of my work in the neighborhood, I knocked on a door on Berkshire Avenue. A young couple came to the door and invited me to come in. When I inquired about any problems or concerns they had about their community, they took me to their small backyard, where they had hung out their laundry to dry. As we examined a white sheet on the clothes line, we could see specks of carbon clinging to it.

We went back inside, and I listened to their concerns about the leather factory on the nearby shore of Lake Ontario. We agreed that pollution from the factory was the likely cause of their problem.

The next morning at our staff meeting in the Riverdale office, I spoke about what I had seen and learned the previous night. As result, we immediately formed a pollution committee. The young couple and their neighbors got involved.

We made an appointment with the owner of the factory. As a delegation of concerned neighbors, we met with him to negotiate for the installation of an improved filtration system at the factory. Our organizing for cultural action was successful, and the factory was equipped with a new filtration system. Happily, after that, pollutants no longer fell on members of the Riverdale community.

Phase IV: Reorganizing/Conscientization

Both Alinsky and Freire viewed their work as bringing things to a collective whole. For Alinsky, compassion and justice were accomplished through community organization, by bringing people together to develop a community of action. The old structures that were at the service of justice were transformed by newly created structures. The old and the new structures were woven together into a fabric for justice making. This was called the *reorganizing* phase. Whether expressed in a town hall meeting, a union gathering, or even a political convention, something exciting happened when people gathered to express their collective energy for justice.

For Freire, the process of transformation culimated with *conscientization*. By this he meant that the combination of reflection and action is essential for transformation to occur, and for people and structures to undergo meaningful change. He wrote that communities should engage in a process of discovery and transformation that "cannot be purely intellectual but must involve action; nor can it be limited to mere activism, but must include serious reflection."

It is important to recognize that as instruments of transformation, we are involved in that transformation. We, too, go through phases—whether we name them as Alinsky or Freire did, or whether we name them more in line with our current concept of geo-justice. We move from apathy to hope, from hope to letting go, from letting go to creativity and to applying the energy of creativity in ways that change us and our societal relationships.

I believe that the local component of geo-justice depends on imagination and courage. It is not merely learned in a classroom or from a book. Rather, it is written in our lives. It is conceived out of struggle. We learn it by getting up each morning and putting ourselves on the line against the forces that would hold us back. It is grasped in the struggle of constant effort, of moving ourselves (and others) from where we are to where we want to be.

A Starting Point for Local Action

I remember an event that marked the beginnings of my organizing experience. My older brother was the best pitcher on our baseball team. I wasn't playing much, so he and I convinced our manager that I should catch when my brother pitched. This was my first organizing project, my first experience of being involved in shifting patterns of relationship to achieve a desired result.

Later, as a student of Saul Alinsky, I became excited about the opportunity to learn more about how to empower the poor and disadvantaged. Remembering how I solved the problem of not playing enough on my local baseball team, I applied what I had learned to my justice work. I looked for others with whom to play the game of justice: people with influence to whom I could listen, and with whom I could work.

My experience in community organization was liberating. In Toronto, a delegation of community people went to City Hall to meet with the commissioner of public works, who had consistently refused to cooperate with the neighborhood people. Residents were outraged at the number of tickets they were getting for parking on streets near their homes. They wanted to organize to obtain affordable permits for overnight parking. When the leader of our delegation presented our concerns and received the commissioner's promise to come to a community meeting, the people felt excited and empowered. They felt, perhaps for the first time, that they had been heard and they had some influence over their lives.

Listening and Recognition

The local component of geo-justice starts with listening and recognition. Listening is the most profound act of recognition we can extend to another. To act with integrity, we must observe what is going on. As Freire is fond of saying, we must "become wet with the soul of the people." Similarly, Pope Francis says that those who serve the people should be like "shepherds living with the smell of the sheep." Then—and only then—can we act prophetically. As fields are planted and plowed to be planted again, so listening and recognizing continuously call forth the new from the old, birth from death, and development from decline.

This approach creates solidarity and common ground—the capacity to act from within our deepest aspirations. We begin to see "the world itself as a living being, made up of dynamic aspects," as eco-feminist author Starhawk writes, where "all things have inherent value [and are] interrelated in patterns."

Thus, this component of geo-justice grounds us in the everyday fabric of our existence. As we learn to listen, we recognize our place in the cosmic scheme of things. Our efforts are punctuated by epiphanies; that is, our work is informed by our capacity to experience the divine. Though it is expressed in concrete action, the local component acknowledges mystery because it simultaneously roots us in the Earth and enhances an appreciation of our place as sacred space.

A Faith-Based Approach

Today the work of community organization has taken on a faith-based perspective in many places. In line with this approach, some cities have organized coalitions of congregations representing different denominations to bring about justice in their local area. This can be a more effective structure than the traditional labor-intensive approach of bringing neighborhood organizations together around a list of specific local issues—such as parking, green space, pollution, education, and issues for young people.

Here in California, we have witnessed community organizations make major contributions to the struggle for justice by adopting approaches that were developed by leaders who were able to find their own ways to create concrete solutions. One example is the program now known as the PICO National

Network, which was founded by John Baumann, SJ. When a community issue surfaced that called out for a response, the leaders decided that the best way to find a solution would be to use the local congregations or churches as their base. As a result of this conversation, a new approach to community organization was launched.

Process Reflection: Acting Locally

In the words of Pope Francis, "An authentic faith—which is never comfortable or completely personal—always involves a deep desire to change the world, to transmit values, to leave this earth somehow better than we found it." Acting locally can begin with as few as one or two people. When you want to take action, it helps to clarify your focus and intentions with a small group. Discuss what you see as important and what you might do about it. Then you can move into a larger community setting. You can also use social media to enhance the work of integral ecology with a planetary perspective.

1. Spend fifteen minutes with a partner doing the following:
2. Tell each other what you see as your community's most pressing need.
3. Listen to each other's different perspectives.
4. Reflect on the relative priority of needs emerging from this conversation.
5. What initial action can you agree upon to take personally and/or together in response to the greatest need?
6. In what ways do you understand organization to be the first act of justice making?

Do the following with a group (no more than eight members) facing a local issue to be resolved.

1. Draw a blank pie chart on a white board with eight slices.
2. Have each person inscribe a short phrase on one pie piece that represents what they think should be done.
3. Discuss the proposed actions.
4. Each person has two votes that must be recorded on two different pie slices. Count up the votes and use this information to decide on the priorities of actions to be taken.

Busy

Every day when the sun comes up,
birds flap their wings,
cars speed through the street,
carrying passengers
hurriedly to another day's work.

Some mornings
we awake with anxiety and worry,
gripped by expectation
and emptiness.

Yet each morning
is a new beginning,
an adventure awaiting,
nudging us to the edge of expectation,
beyond all uncertainty and doubt.

Chapter 6

Interiority and Depth: The Psycho-Social Component

New emphasis [is] put on recognition of spirituality and transcendental needs as intrinsic aspects of human nature and on the right of every individual to pursue his or her own spiritual path.

—**Stan Grof** (*Ancient Wisdom and Modern Science*, p. vii, 1985)

The psychology of a person has a profound impact on how that person acts in society. In our city streets, and even in remote areas—such as the far north of Canada's Saskatchewan province—the alarming rise in violence in classrooms, subways, theaters, and offices has reached epidemic proportions. While background checks and other common sense regulations are needed, it is also important that we focus on those who shoot others and examine the emotional well-being of those who perpetuate such crimes.

We live in a culture of anxiety. Many struggle with being unemployed or underemployed, while others are stressed by working two or more jobs just to make ends meet. The news is filled with reports about the latest terror attack in the Middle East or even in our own neighborhood. Black parents fear their sons will be gunned down in the streets. Hispanic children fear their parents will be deported and their families split up. Muslims and others fear they will be insulted, ostracized, or worse. At the same time, white people are anxious, as author Toni Morrison says, because they sense their "conviction of their natural superiority is being lost."

Anxiety and fear flourish when people feel threatened, alienated, or marginalized. This in turn leads to violent outbreaks and the irretrievable loss of life. We may not singlehandedly be able to stop the violence, but there is a growing need to think about how we can address it at our doorsteps. We need to develop support groups and other organizations that can connect us as neighbors. We have to look within our own hearts, as well as do our best to connect with others on that level.

I often ask friends, "What are you thinking?" This question is prompted by my wish to have access to their interior depths. This is where we have our reservoirs of inexhaustible energies. These energies are a powerful source for bringing about the birth of the new culture that we envision. Our immediate challenge is to awaken our interior sensitivities to experience more fully the beauty, mystery, darkness, and dynamic balance of the Earth. From these recesses of human self-awareness will flow the organization and actions to heal the wounds of the Earth and its people.

Many of the things I have pursued over the years were motivated by a desire to understand my inner life more fully. I participated in therapy, spiritual community, cultural work, and sometimes friendship for this purpose. I was striving, often unknowingly, to make conscious the story, the myth that lived within me. I have come to understand that knowing my own story and discovering my own myth is an important part of becoming a new person in a culture in the throes of a paradigm shift. Jean Shinoda Bolen writes, "When knowledge of the mythic dimension comes into your possession, it can help you find your bearings and a path that is true for you, one that reflects who you authentically are."

One way of talking about the new myth for our time is to

say that our goal is to make it possible for the story of Earth to be the story of our culture on Earth. The myth, the story of this new relationship with Earth, makes the energies of the cosmos available in cultural form; interiority and depths are important dimensions of Earth story.

Internalizing the Mystery

When scientists discovered evidence of the origin of the universe, they said that these seeds of the cosmic fireball were like the "footprints" of God. When we connect to the deepest recesses of our interior life, we also find ourselves in touch with the divine. A friend said, "When I go into the ravine to participate in the restoration of the creek, flowers, and trees, I know that I am healing a dimension of myself that if ignored and left alone would become much like that neglected field." A wise woman of years said to me that throughout her life she had seen a blade of grass as a manifestation of the divine: "In response to the sun and rain it becomes green and tall in the spring; it is a sign of the resurrection. It is of Earth as we are; it has deep, strong roots that reach into Earth."

These women, like many other people, have a cellular relationship with the Earth. Each sees her true self as a dimension of Earth, as an ecological self. They see the Earth as not mine but me. They see healing as a personal, social, and planetary event, a balancing of the inner and the outer from the place where we experience an interconnectedness with the Earth.

Thomas Merton was fond of saying that he never felt more connected with his brother monks in the monastery than when he was in solitude. We are interconnected and in communion with the natural world. From this perspective our questions become "Who am I?" and "What am I becoming?" We must decide that before we can address the next question: "What am I going to do?" As one woman said, "Maybe I can't save the rain forest, but I can save the tree in my backyard." By seeing ourselves as a dimension of the Earth, we see more and more how the poor of Earth—the homeless, those marginalized by sexual orientation, income, race, mental illness, and other forms of oppression—are themselves connected with the suffering of the poor Earth.

The awareness of this new story of the Earth resides within the depths of the human psyche and within the entire Earth community. Just as there are galaxies in the cosmos and trees, birds, and oceans on the Earth, so also our interior life is a realm of incredible vastness. In our deep inner knowing, we are liberated from consciousness of isolatoin and separateness. We view our interior life from the perspective of the cosmos, not the confines of our human experience.

As we live with the Earth, so also in a very real way the Earth lives within us. Our lives are nourished by the internalized mystery of beauty. When we feel the power of the ocean, the tenacity of a mountain lion, the tenderness of a child, and the wisdom of an older person, we have been touched by the beauty of our living Earth. In the grand canyons and galactic constellations of our interior life we are nourished by avenues of wisdom; the memory of blue skies; the power of the magnificent trees of courage; the serenity of a gentle breeze; and the strength of rich, dark soil.

When we internalize our experience of the mystery of the Earth, we undergo a psychic photosynthesis. Photosynthesis transforms and incarnates the energy of the remote sun. In psychic photosynthesis, we ingest and make the mystery of the cosmos part of our interior life. We not only consume the

Earth, but our psychic inner life is shaped by the Earth in ways that are deeply mysterious. In fact, we incarnate the Earth in our hearts and minds. We have a deep mystical connection with the Earth. We become open and vulnerable to what the Earth is saying to us. The Earth's story gives expression to the meaning and purpose of our lives. We learn to listen more fully to our inner voice, a voice that speaks to us through the seas, the sky, and the trees. We experience a renewed sense of the sacred and the mystery that lives within us.

A Shift in Consciousness

Being involved in the revolutionary work of community organization during the 1970s was exciting, empowering, and productive, yet I was troubled at times by what seemed more like inversion than conversion. I saw have-nots become the haves. I saw people achieve the ability to act. This was very rewarding. Their actions achieved a solution to the issues they had identified. But it was clear that something was lacking. I was concerned that there seemed to be no corresponding interior change. There was an exchange of power, yet no deeper change. Since then, I have learned that the power of domination can be transformed into an ability to act fully from within and among the entire Earth community.

North American culture has, generally speaking, enshrined the rights of the individual at the expense of society. However, geo-justice rejects the either/or dichotomy between the individual and the group. Instead, it asserts both/and. By refusing the either/or trap that forces us to choose between individual and social, personal and cultural, we can better align ourselves with the goal of societal healing.

An important dimension of working for justice with the

Earth is a shift in consciousness. As our awareness of the Earth deepens, we often undergo profound changes. An increasing number of people tell me they now see their connection to the Earth as the basis for their spiritual journey. They begin to view themselves, others, and the Earth in a new way.

This new consciousness is enhanced by making the connection between personal experience and the Earth's experience. The dialectic contributes to a new self-understanding. It supports a consciousness that is both transformative and transforming. This shift in awareness brings a new understanding of ourselves and the world.

When the congregation of cardinals of the Church gathered in Rome in 2013 to elect the next pope, each cardinal was given five minutes to speak. The brief proclamation of the Archbishop of Argentina—soon to become Pope Francis—lasted three and a half minutes. It not only electrified the crowd, but also became a significant moment that led to his election. It was as if he were familiar with the work of Christopher Lasch, who wrote about the culture of narcissism, when he spoke: "The only purpose of the Church is to go out to tell the world the good news about Jesus Christ…" He continued, "The Church had gotten too wrapped up in itself. It was too navel gazing. It had become 'self-referential,' which had made it sick. It was suffering a kind of theological narcissism."

He continued, "The Church is supposed to be the *mysterium lunae*—the mystery of the moon is that it has no light but simply reflects the light of the sun. The Church must not fool itself that it has light of its own…. The next pope should be someone who helps the Church surge forth to the peripheries like a sweet and comforting mother who offers the joy of Jesus to the world."

And now he has become that pope. He is exemplifying the

psycho-social dimension of geo-justice, which focuses on the connection between the person and society.

When we perceive problems through a self-referential lens, or as either insoluble or nonexistent, we can lapse into despair, apathy, and resignation. Rather than create solutions, we act out our unresolved problems. We create nuclear stockpiles or we compel the good Earth to do our will with massive doses of fertilizer and ever-more powerful machinery.

The energy of our new awareness must be invested in transforming ourselves as well as macro structures and systems. We need both local and global perspectives, to unite our personal pain to the Earth's pain. Psychic healing becomes a microcosm of the healing of society. When we see the individual psyche linked with all of humanity and with the entire cosmos, every aspect of our lives becomes an instrument of planetary peace. Separateness and fragmentation are brought into balance.

From the perspective of geo-justice, the psyche's dynamic relationship to society integrates our fragmented inner life to promote inner harmony and planetary peace.

Emotional Integration

Historically, psychology and medicine have opted for the Cartesian and Newtonian paradigms; that is, a mechanical model of the universe. Once set in motion, the universe was seen as operating like a machine made up of many parts. The machine broke down only when a part failed. According to this view, healing happens when the part is repaired independently of the whole.

Psychology and medicine have traditionally assumed that the body and mind operate in a similar way. Mechanically understood, body and mind draw attention to themselves only when they are out of order. Mental health in this context idealizes tranquility and the *absence* of strong emotion. Even today, psychiatric hospitals depend on drug therapy to suppress (tranquilize) patients' feelings.

By contrast, geo-justice values the healing potential of emotion. A geo-justice psychology affirms Freud's approach of making the unconscious conscious, Jung's concept of befriending our shadow, and Robert Linder's assertion that personal psychological processes are instruments of cultural evolution.

Dr. Stan Grof, the prophetic psychiatrist, suggests that release of the trapped energies of the psyche can foster a spiritual emergence. Grof suggests that the psyche itself is coextensive with the universe. In *Beyond the Brain* he writes, "Modem consciousness research has added new levels, realms, and dimensions and shows the human psyche as being essentially commensurate with the whole universe and all of existence."

Carl Jung, in an interview with Laurens van der Post on the BBC, commented: "When you look inside yourself, you see the universe and all its stars in all their infinity, objectively spaced out, and you fall away into an infinite symmetry, an infinite objective mystery within yourself, as great as the one without!"

When we can feel the pain of the Earth and identify it as our own pain, we can recognize that the psyche, in working towards its own healing and harmony, moves us all toward planetary justice, balance and peace.

Toward Unity and Wholeness

Even as we experience the transformation of our worldview, we are developing a new framework for understanding the psyche. Spectrum psychology, as articulated by Ken Wilber, envisages the psyche functioning in four different ways, or channels. Each of these channels provides an avenue through which the organism can heal itself.

- Sensory awakening is the activation and experiencing of all the senses.
- Biographical exploration is healing through remembering and reliving our experiences.
- Perinatal processing is the experience before, during, and after birth, and the passage to new levels of experience.
- Transpersonal work is moving beyond the confines of space and time, transcending the limited range of the senses as the source of knowledge.

Stan Grof developed an approach to activating the healing properties of the psyche that he calls *holonomic integration*. The name means moving toward unity and wholeness. It combines enhanced breathing with evocative music, focused body work, mandala drawing, and group sharing. This healing approach invites us simply to be, to support and to allow.

My own participation in holonomic integration was one of the most healing experiences of my life. I also found it to be very helpful in assisting others to experience deep levels of transformation. Their comments demonstrate how, given the right conditions, the psyche can experience healing.

- The time passed very quickly. I wasn't aware of it passing.

- At the end, I was very silent, very centered, and did not want to do anything but just be quiet and centered. I was quite full when I left the experience.

- I felt deeply the various moods of music—sometimes stimulated to a very intense energy that I allowed my body to express as impelled; otherwise to a profound peace and restfulness. The overall effect seemed to be one of a sense of wholeness and contentment with who I am in the cosmos.

- I was going through some conflicts before the process, and at the end of it the conflicts seemed negligible. Also got in touch with a certain anger toward my dad—that got dissolved, and now I feel a real closeness with him. It seems as if we're on a new plane of relationship.

These statements indicate that in such a process, spirituality and healing coincide. Together, they confirm that our inner psychological experience is dialectically connected to our social experience. Thus, the psyche can be a source of geo-justice.

What We Do to Ourselves, We Do to the Earth

The many new approaches to psychology now available have enormous potential for balance and harmony with the Earth. To take just one example, research about the perinatal process has revealed that the experience of being trapped in the birth process evokes emotions that can later find expression in war. The task of psychology, as an instrument of geo-justice, is the creation of a safe place to detoxify our emotional poisons without harm to others or the Earth.

In this view of the psyche, it is possible both to experience emotions fully and to contribute to transforming the planet. Self-exploration and expression will cleanse, purify, and protect both ourselves and the planet. We will be less likely to act out hidden emotions. We will be able to mend the inner fragmentation of our lives and our alienation from the Earth. We will be able to experience each moment fully, without always having to move on to more ambitious plans and unlimited growth. We will move from compulsion to peace.

I believe that the examination of one's emotional life is extremely important. What troubles me is seeing therapy and community organizing in isolation. When considered apart, each fails to encompass the wisdom available from the other. One pursues emotional healing while overlooking oppressive structures, and the other seeks systemic change without dealing with personal need. I feel we need to integrate the psycho-social component into the geo-justice paradigm.

The psycho-social dimension of geo-justice invites us to recognize ourselves in relation to society. What we do to ourselves, we do to others and to the Earth. The alternative is equally true: as psychology transforms how we think, live, and act, it becomes an instrument for geo-justice.

Process Reflection: Transforming Self and Earth

Pope Francis urges us to become "channels through which God can water the earth, protect all creation, and make justice and peace flourish." You can become such a channel by exploring the psycho-social component of geo-justice. This exercise incorporates both exploration on your own through journal writing as well as in small group discussion.

1. Writing in your journal, ponder the following questions:
    *   In what ways do I lead my life as a liberating process that brings healing to the Earth and its people?
    *   How does my experience of the natural world show me that the creative power of the universe is the primary source of divine revelation?
    *   How do I ensure that my actions are congruent with my beliefs?
    *   How does this reflection enhance my understanding of the psycho-social component of geo-justice?

2. In small groups, ponder the following questions:
    *   What in your life ignites your imagination and interest?
    *   What do you see as the relationship between personal change and societal transformation?
    *   How do you see transformation in yourself contributing to transformation at the community level and stewardship of the Earth?
    *   What systems and structures in society (e.g., industry, politics) restrict your freedom of personal transformation?

High Perches/Low Aspirations

Isolated people
sitting on high stools,
seemingly espousing
low aspirations
for their lives.

Gazing into a silver tube,
belching out the venom
of a failed leadership
of a previously promised land,
from these high perches,
unreflected awareness
seems to ooze out and
spill into an ever-darkening room.

Chapter 7

Communion and Compassion: The Global Component

Relationship is the essence of existence.
> —**Thomas Berry and Brian Swimme** (*The Universe Story*, pp. 77-78, 1992)

Questions about justice and compassion have been the most engaging and sometimes the most puzzling of any I have attempted to address in my life. On occasion, I have asked myself whether my Irish heritage—a culture widely known for being anti-government and resilient in the face of oppression—contributed to my impulse to work for the underdog, to be on the side of the poor. Whatever the reason, I have always found myself on the side of the marginalized and disadvantaged.

I have noticed that although compassion is the litmus test and culminating touchstone of a spirituality that is aligned with geo-justice, it is often misunderstood and neglected. It has frequently been my experience that justice is not well understood in relationship to an evolutionary view of the world.

Not only are we troubled by the pain of social and ecological injustice, but we are also troubled by the approaches taken to heal injustice. We have lost the focus of "joy the gospel" that Pope Francis champions, and become preoccupied with judgment rather than mercy. Many who take up the work for justice too readily abandon that work, feeling discouraged. Guilt and a misguided obligation have parched their spirit and contracted their vision. On occasion, marriages and personal health are sacrificed on the altar of community. Once I was asked to encourage a man to run for the presidency of a community organization. But then I learned that his marriage was breaking up. Something was wrong in his approach: his work for justice had become itself an act of injustice. Too often, justice work has overlooked the interior life. Many justice workers do not feel nourished in their efforts to liberate the oppressed.

I have heard friends and colleagues report that their efforts toward social justice have left them fragmented and alienated. Given this experience, they retreat. But work for justice can be done with a different perspective. The work of compassion can be an adventure in communion. It can best be understood in relationship to the universe as an intimate presence and as a response to the supreme challenge of extending love and relationship to self, others, and Earth.

The Quest for Communion and Compassion

Alinsky said there can be no true revolution (structural change) without an accompanying reformation (internal change). I understood this principle, but nevertheless was troubled when I saw communities that previously were alive for change lack the sense of community and compassion that had brought their organizing efforts into existence in the first place. A classic example is the Back of the Yards project in the Chicago neighborhood where Alinsky did his first major work by bringing justice to the world of industrial workers in the 1940s. Alinsky was able to translate the principles he had learned from his mentor, John L. Lewis of the United Mine Workers of America and apply them in an urban setting. The Back of the Yards project was a significant example of democracy. Great things were accomplished as compassionate community relationships were fostered and built. However, Alinsky also learned about the inevitable diminishing of energy that occurs in community organizing. He concluded that an organizing effort will lose sight of its original purpose after five to eight years. So it was with Back of the Yards project. Years later, I visited the area and saw that it had become an embarrassingly racist community.

While puzzling over this, I inaugurated a project called the Institute for Communities in Canada, at Humber College in Toronto. Instinctively, I felt that Paulo Freire's work would provide the answers I needed. My understanding of justice changed when I read his words: "Trusting the people is the indispensable precondition for revolutionary change. A real humanist can be identified more by his trust in the people, which engages him in their struggle, than by a thousand actions in their favour, without that trust." Trust is the foundation of communion and compassion. Without it, we cannot heal ourselves, our communities, or our planet.

As we courageously open our hearts to the pain of our planet, which we experience as our own, we respond to the impulse to participate in the healing properties of our living Earth. As instruments of communion and compassion, we become present with love and kindness to envelop the Earth community in an experience of mutual belonging.

When I discovered this spirituality of the Earth, I began to view justice in a new way. It was a spirituality that extended into the natural world. The Earth itself became a context for justice making. I began to see that justice can be experienced as communion and compassion.

Communion is not a private undertaking, but the central fabric of all our lives. Through communion and compassion, we participate in an event that is already occurring. Thomas Merton speaks of this when he addresses his fellow monks:

"My dear brothers, we are already one. But we imagine that we are not. And what we have to discover is our original unity. What we have to be is what we already are."

Within the universe there is a comprehensive bonding, a compassionate embrace that brings everything into relationship with everything else. This mysterious energy celebrates relatedness and heals alienation. This cosmic communion finds expression in the tapestry of an interconnected culture. It makes possible a relatedness that is beyond what we previous imagined.

The Earth can be a powerful instrument of compassion. Of course there are times when nature seems harsh or destructive. Yet if we look at the bigger picture, we see that the Earth also has a way of rebalancing and healing itself. After a hillside is ravaged by fire, for example, new plants sprout quickly and their roots help prevent landsides. We see many relationships that can teach us about balance, harmony, and peace. As I contemplated this, being part of a community of compassion made sense to me. Compassion is about experiencing communion, about bonding and extending our capacity for relationship. I had read Meister Eckhart's words, "Compassion means justice…. The person who understands what I have to say about justice understands everything I have to say." I began to see more fully what he meant.

Compassion is woven into the fabric of life. It is ultimately who I believe we are, and what the Earth is and does. As the Earth is coded for compassion, so are we. The words of the civil rights' anthem—"We shall overcome… We'll walk hand in hand… We shall live in peace"—made new and even more sense to me. Compassion is about the energy that draws us together in love. Dr. King eloquently articulated this when he said, "In a real sense all life is interrelated. All [people] are caught in an inescapable network of mutuality, tied in a single garment of destiny."

After a young man killed nine African-American members of a Bible study group in Charleston, South Carolina, the survivors went to the killer's hearing to express their forgiveness. This courageous act earned their church a Nobel Peace Prize nomination. One of the church members said, "The mere fact that the church is in the same realm as Mahatma Gandhi or Martin Luther King Jr. is one of the highest honors."

Compassion adds a new dimension to justice making. Justice making is not a human desire for rearranging priorities and realigning power, as important as these may be. The Earth is constantly renewing itself. Flowers are blooming, rivers are flowing, photosynthesis continues to happen. As humans, we are invited to remove the social and ecological obstacles that destroy the Earth's creativity and to be courageous artists of our own lives. For too long, I believed that justice is the mechanical realignment of power and money. Eventually, I realized that the Earth is a living, interconnected system. Our role as humans is to participate in this system of relationships. Our participation can contribute to harmony and balance; it can be an experience and expression of compassion that points inevitably toward geo-justice.

At this time in history, many institutions are ailing; they are not participating in compassion. In fact, their collapse has created a lot of anger and frustration. The Earth is telling us something we need to hear. The annihilation of species and resources and the ecological threat of planetary destruction reveal the enormous need we have for a new perspective on justice. Compassion with regard for the Earth is our agenda for today and our hope for tomorrow.

Much as I had learned that the psyche has properties for

healing, I also discovered that the Earth is resilient and self-healing. As I reflected on the cycle by which the sun, water, and earth give life to the pear tree, which in turn provides food for the hungry, I celebrated the powerful healing dynamics of the Earth and began to examine more fully the meaning of cultural rebirth. The Earth becomes our teacher. We celebrate and acknowledge the way in which newness and life are infused into every drop of water, the atomic energy in every grain of sand, the divine goodness reflected in a gentle breeze.

Developing compassion and communion also draws us into a deeper appreciation of the pain and oppression that are imposed on our planet. We feel more connected to the poor in Guatemala and to the rainforest in Brazil. Out of the cosmic crucifixion of the Earth, creativity and newness abound. As we participate in the planet's creativity, we become what Hildegard of Bingen calls a "flowering orchard." Perhaps the most important task of our time is to fashion a web of relationships to heal separation and promote interdependence, to bring about compassion in the culture.

In the work of geo-justice, no separation exists between the personal and the planetary. There is a direct connection, for example, between the crack in the ozone layer and the crack that is sold in the streets. There is an indelible connection between social injustice and ecological devastation. The destruction of a human life by cocaine and the destruction of the atmosphere by hydrocarbons are one act.

Compassion is about extending our capacity for relationship toward both the atmosphere and the street. When alienation is transformed into community, isolation into uniqueness, when people feel honored for who they are, and when they are listened to, healing will happen. When images, stories, and myths express communion and compassion, the culture will be born anew.

The Earth's Invitation to Compassion

It is my experience that institutional bureaucrats often do not want to meet with people about whom they have to make decisions. Repeatedly, when they do agree to meet people and develop relationships, they act differently. They become more compassionate. In a similar way, ecological justice will blossom when bureaucrats—and all people—are closer to the natural world. If we walk on the Earth and are touched by the beauty of a flower, the rhapsody of a bird's song, and the delicious gurgle of a brook, we are more likely to treat the Earth with reverence. When we celebrate the sacredness of the Earth and see there the God who is in all things, we truly have a basis for compassion. We will then know the Earth as our spiritual home, a place of revelation where communion is experienced and made known.

Compassion is a sacred, intimate relationship; it is love. To act justly is to create loving communion with a spouse, the ocean, a tree. When we extend our love for a person and a place into the classroom, the board room, the bedroom, the legislature, and nature, we are engaged in compassion. As we fall in love and internalize the mystery of relatedness, we extend our embrace to the Earth. The book of nature reveals that the Earth is our sacred home.

The work of communion and compassion supports the harmony and balance already present in the Earth. It supports the self-healing properties of the Earth. As we remove the illusion of separateness, we learn from the Earth about love. The Earth does not condemn a river that floods or reject a volcano for erupting. It does not punish a fungus or virus for its mere existence. Rather, communion and compassion heal the aneurysms and the ruptures in creation.

Compassion is at the heart of the Christian tradition and constitutive to the gospel. Nevertheless, in practice, there has been a separation between personal piety and social engagement. As a result, too often, justice makers have been in the minority. A spirituality of the Earth will support a more inclusive approach to justice making.

Our invitation is to fall in love with ourselves and with each other, the Earth, and the cosmos; to become vulnerable, open, and connected.

To practice communion and compassion is to stop putting poison in our bodies or burying toxins in the ground, and to support ecological practices, such as reforestation, that purify the soil, air, and water.

There is a direct relationship between our destiny and compassion. Compassion, the full engagement in life, provides a window of opportunity into the next step in our life. By engaging fully in the culture to change it, we achieve a new understanding and appreciation of the universe and the dynamic patterns that reveal its deeper meaning.

The Power of Mysticism

Mysticism refers to the experience of oneness. It is about awe, beauty, and wonder. In the context of geo-justice, it enables us to feel united to the Earth as a whole and to know our place within it.

Nourished by mysticism, our awareness moves from individual rights or national sovereignty toward a planetary perspective. Instead of "me" or "my family" or "my country," we start to think of a world community and a planetary culture.

This community finds expression in political and economic organizations that serve a new global civilization. Instead of defending ourselves by separating from others, we work toward a world order that transcends national differences.

As the planetary crisis intensifies, global mysticism becomes a vehicle for healing the devastation that surrounds us. We are global citizens reflecting on ourselves and on the world. We examine political, cultural, and economic dimensions so that we can transform them. We are, in that sense, healers. And at the same time, we are ourselves in need of healing.

Marshall McLuhan was perhaps the first to refer to our planet as a global village. He was primarily interested in the communication technologies that make information exchange possible anywhere on the planet. In many ways, he predicted what we now experience as our daily technical reality. But he also implied a planetary consciousness that enables us to recognize ourselves as part of the whole. Our consciousness can envelop the Earth. This awareness of the Earth as a whole is analogous to seeing global weather patterns. When we watch cloud patterns swirling over the Earth in a satellite image, we know that what affects us also affects others considerable distances away.

This global consciousness shifts our approach to the Earth from domination to community. Thomas Berry writes, "Our spirituality is Earth derived—the thoughts and emotions, the social forms and rituals of the human community are as much Earth as is the soil and the rocks and the trees and the flowers."

This awareness of our oneness with the Earth promotes the kind of perspective required for geo-justice. As humans, we are what Berry refers to as the psyche of the universe and the consciousness of the world. The Earth becomes aware of itself through the self-reflective consciousness of the human.

Our role as the consciousness of the Earth creates a climate for global questioning and engagement.

We need a global approach to problems and issues. That approach needs to be energized by a mystical consciousness. The mystical component for justice making underlines the need for an enhanced awareness of planetary interdependence. This interdependence affects all life forms, from microbes to tropical forests to political and economic systems. This awareness complements and supports major shifts in our worldview, and reinforces the image of the Earth as sacred.

I believe that this kind of global mysticism is emerging. Projects for justice and peace increasingly adopt a world perspective. Human rights organizations cut across national boundaries to encourage global systems of justice. Moment by moment, the focus on information and support on a planetary scale increases. This direction is a concrete basis for hope. It taps into the transformation needed at all levels of existence.

A Global Coalition

Geo-justice gives birth to our fondest hopes for the planet. This hope provides a window of opportunity for a truly global network and for a process that will integrate existing networks as partners in a Pentecost for the planet.

The first task for leaders of this global event is to develop imaginative ways to translate the vision of geo-justice into the lives of all people on this planet. We are called to quilt together a tapestry of relationships that some would call a cosmic fire-web, and that is autonomous, interconnected, and self-organizing. We need what Thomas Berry has called "a human way of entering into the rhythms of the universe."

Pope Francis understands the vital place of community and

interconnectedness in our lives. When asked why he was drawn to the Jesuits, he pointed to the importance of community in his own life, saying, "I was always looking for a community. I did not see myself as a priest on my own. I need a community."

Most people have traditionally viewed what happens to them as having significance only in their own lives. They need a perspective that sees cultural and personal events as expressions of the dynamics of the universe itself. They need to develop a cosmological imagination. This is a transformation of enormous magnitude. I believe the beginning of this transformation is already happening all around the world. Leaders are called to promote and nurture what is already taking place.

Through this process, we are reminded that we are not alone, and that people around the world share our hopes and dreams for the welfare of the planet. This process is already giving birth to an entirely different kind of organization, comprised of informal networks of information, support, and common action. Through these networks, we are developing new ways of seeing and acting in the world. This movement is ushering in a new era, a conscious shift toward peace for the planet. The Earth Summits and the Paris Agreement, as well Pope Francis's *Laudato Si'*, are examples of this growing global momentum.

We need a more mature spirituality to respond to the challenge of this new era of global interdependence. Instead of strengthening individual nations, we need to build structures for planetary peace. We need nothing less than a new world order. Such an order will respond compassionately to the brokenness of peoples, the woundedness of nations, and the suffering of the Earth.

The Earth is the ground of the new world order. It is a biocracy that is truly democratic, and in which every species has a voice. To move toward this new world order, we must follow the guidance of Thomas Berry, who says, "We cannot discover ourselves without first discovering the universe, the Earth, and the imperatives of our own being. Each of these has a creative power and a vision far beyond any rational thought or cultural creation of which we are capable. Nor should we think of these as isolated from our own individual being or from the human community. We have no existence except within the Earth and within the universe."

Justice is no longer merely a moral obligation, but rather a deep communion with all that is, and with the planet itself.

Process Reflection: The Work of Compassion

Meister Eckhart wrote, "Compassion means justice." It is up to each of us to understand what form this takes in our lives and our communities, and in the world at large. This exercise can be done alone or in a group.

1. How does the Earth's expression of harmony, balance, and renewal contribute to your understanding of compassion as an extension of your capacity for relationship with the entire Earth community?

2. How do you understand the presence of cancer, AIDS, political oppression, and all forms of human suffering within our sacred world?

3. Compassion is about both reformation (internal, personal change) and revolution (structural, societal change). What practical steps can you take to become more compassionate?

4. How do the dynamics of compassion, as outlined in this chapter, provide a framework for your efforts in justice making?

5. Have you experienced some approaches to justice to be themselves unjust?

Process Reflection: Spiral Ritual

The spiral as a symbol dates back to ancient times when people noticed that the stars spun around a central point in the sky. Today we know from science that our planet exists within a spiral galaxy. The spiral is also sometimes taken as a symbol of the divine feminine. In this group exercise, the spiral symbolizes the universe as well as our place within it, and becomes a vehicle through which to express our solidarity with the Earth.

1. Participants join hands and form a circle.
2. The leader releases the hand of the person on his or her left and begins to circle to the right, moving along the outside of the circle, in spiral fashion.
3. The leader greets each person with his or her eyes (without words) as the line of people expands beyond the circle and moves about the room.
4. The leader then reverses direction, with the participants following, and reforms the circle.
5. As the participants stand in the circle again, they chant, "The Earth is our mother, we must take care of her." They celebrate their solidarity with the Earth and all her people.
6. To complete this process, the participants reflect on their experience.

Letter to a Young Poet

Dear young poet,
I write to you today,
you who worry about many things,
feel deeply the pain of the world,
the pain of each other
the pain of the Earth.

Please, young poet,
write about what is inmost in your heart,
about what gives you meaning.
Stay connected to what gives you life.
Compose poems from your heart.
Reach out to friend and foe alike.
Create space where your heart can soar.
Invite others to join you.
At the threshold of each new moment,
say YES:
yes to the world,
yes to the quest.

Arise, dear poet,
to the summit
and the source
of all you long to be.
Blessed be.
Yes, blessed be!

PART III
The Paschal Mystery in our Midst

Chapter 8
This Incarnational Moment: Awakening to Geo-Justice

Today let us remember these three words: newness, harmony, and mission.
> —**Pope Francis** (Homily, Saint Peter's Square, Pentecost Sunday, May 19, 2013)

In these early years of the twenty-first century, we can look back and review the defining events of yesterday that have brought us to this moment. Among them are the free speech movement, the early Earth Day celebrations, the civil rights and Black lives matter movements, the occupy movement, and the realization that it is possible to dissolve oppressive webs of power and make tomorrow better than today. We ask how these ideas and movements have prepared us to face uncertainty and not be deterred.

As Christians we also ask, "Who is Jesus today? Who is this Jesus of the universe and Earth, this divine one who was cosmically present at the beginning of the universe, this man of mercy and compassion who broke through into human/Earth history in the manger of Bethlehem, and brought joy to the sorrowful and vision to the spiritually blind?"

What does this divine person who altered the course of history and changed the lives of so many say to us today? What is his dream for a better world, and how can we expand His vision so that every child, tree, river, and flower is welcome and belongs?

In *Laudato Si'*, Pope Francis invites us to reflect on the gaze of Jesus to bring peace and joy to the world.

As we explore the place of Jesus in our lives, we review our early encounters with the signs and symbols that "the word was made flesh and dwelt among us." We recall the Jesus of our childhood manifest in the plaster image of the (God/human) child in a crèche on Christmas morning. We reflect on his childhood as a carpenter's son, when he taught in the temple and amazed the elders with a wisdom far beyond his years. We recall him as an adult when he taught his disciples, fed the hungry with loaves and fishes, calmed the waters in the stormy sea, gave sight to the blind, and healed the afflicted.

Today we see Jesus as a companion in the struggle against oppression, as a liberator who can heal gun violence, chronic unemployment, and the ills of our cities. We look to re-imagine the lilies in the field so we can celebrate and care for creation, and make possible a community of mercy wherein life is cherished, the vulnerable defended, and the natural world celebrated as a tapestry of beauty and magnificence.

The Defining Moment of the Christian Story

The Christian tradition gives shape and form to our lives. Its dynamics provide the contours of an engaged and meaningful life.

With this in mind, we are able to name the defining moments of the Christian story and describe how to move forward and make possible a life of personal fulfillment and ecological healing.

Our story begins with the incarnation. It is the story of how the invisible God becomes palpably present in human form. Through this incarnational event, the divine within us, Emmanuel, becomes present in our midst. The anointed one enters the world and becomes subject to the joys and sorrow, the hopes, dreams, and disappointments that are the inheritance of what it means to be human.

Joined to this inheritance is the legacy of the gratitude for the new life that is woven into the fabric of everyday existence. Every new day, every flower that blooms, every child born— these are expressions of the incarnation signified by the birth of the Christ child in Bethlehem. This incarnation is now extended wherever there is an infusion of new life born among us.

Through the incarnation we remember the birth of every person, including the poor, the marginalized, and the disconnected. We also turn our attention to the Earth, with its beauty manifest in flowers, rivers and streams, mountain tops and forests. We are also aware of the pain of the planet, the toxic earth, poisoned air, and polluted water.

Woven into the emergent events are accompanying moments of sacrifice. When we speak of sacrifice we invoke its root meaning, which is "to make sacred." Each of us and our companions on the journey will be greeted with the inevitable reality of pain and suffering. Pain may be the result of physical illness or psychic angst or cultural and political turmoil, leading to the need to re-sacrilize the world in which we live.

When we reflect on the experience of Jesus of the cosmos and the cross, our minds are focused on the pain he endured in the Garden of Gethsemane and the crucifixion on Mount Calvary. We receive a powerful lesson about how to respond to the inevitable Gethsemane and Calvary moments in our own lives.

As we allow the pain of the planet and its people to flow into our lives, we are inspired by the ecological impulse alive within us. Empowered by the relentless desire and drive for health and new life, we visualize a vast community of the human and other-than-human worlds rising among us. We imagine and contribute to this vital new community. We see each of our lives moving forward to make a better world possible.

The Vision of Geo-Justice

Like Dr. Martin Luther King, Jr., I have a dream. I dream that this millennium will lead us into a new kind of world. This new era will put us in touch with our origins. It will dissolve alienation and promote creativity and peace. Instead of competing for power over others, we will work together to build a better world by following a vision of beauty, love, laughter, and peace. Our vision will permeate the culture and invite each of us "to do whatever needs to be done."

A friend described this dream as the possibility of a corporate meeting without hierarchy, of winners without losers, of art without elitism, and of living ritual without boredom.

The eyes of children are windows both to our souls and to a new world. In children's eyes, we see our present world reflected; through their eyes, we see our future. Similarly, geo-justice stands as a window to a world that is growing in cohesion and consciousness. The vision of geo-justice lets us see the soul of our own world more clearly, and helps us see what our world must become if it is to survive.

When we look at the world through the eyes of geo-justice, we are challenged. We see the goal, if not all the steps along the way. To reach that goal, we must walk through the labyrinth of our narrowness, sometimes unable to perceive more than one step at a time, trusting that we shall eventually emerge with a renewed vision. The challenge comes in letting go of those areas that imprison our imagination, that lock away our creativity, that prevent us from rising out of our ruts.

Geo-justice is also a doorway for making a cosmic contribution. Doorways open, like opportunities. At this transformational moment, we have a marvelous opportunity. No previous generation has ever had such an opportunity—in part because no previous generation has ever faced such a planetary crisis. Few people even now understand the story of the Earth and their place within it.

Geo-justice offers a vision that enables a new kind of world to happen. A geo-justice class, reflecting on their dreams for the world generated these statements:

- We see a vast evolution of healing in which we participate by giving birth to our deepest passions.
- We see all people and creatures telling their stories and listening to each other.
- We see that the responsibility lies with us.
- We see all people as the human heart of a healthy cosmos, in a new era of love, justice and service.
- We see people waking up to a new vision of creation, where humans will find their place among the species of the Earth and live in peace and harmony with all of creation.
- We see a world without private property laws, fences, and window guards, and instead with welcome signs to all to come and enjoy the Earth.
- We see that the old paradigm is failing, and we are ready for the work of building a new world.
- We see people living and working in harmony with one another.
- We see products produced because they are needed, and as near to the place of consumption as possible.
- We see a precious present.

- We see men and women waking each day to sing their hearts' desire.
- We see God in each other.
- We see work to do.
- We see systems based on true partnership forged by mutual compassion.
- We see all people sharing together in creating a more just world, nurturing the ecology and building a healthy, peaceful future for generations to come.
- We see a world in which all people have ample opportunity to grow to their fullest potential—a world free of war, full of respect and reverence for all creation.

Much of my adult life I have wondered about questions of justice, and how to make our dreams a reality. As an organizer, pastoral worker, and educator, the questions continued to challenge me. What is justice? What do we do about it? What does the doing mean anyway?

Experience teaches us that efforts toward justice and peace are often unsuccessful. Tenants win a victory, only to lose their building. Unions negotiate improved conditions, only to see their plant move to a developing country. Human rights efforts succumb to famine and economic crisis.

Unsuccessful programs and campaigns nudge people to the threshold of despair. Overwhelmed and confused, many no longer believe their efforts will ever make a real difference. My experience has shown that justice work often turns into more of an abstract obligation than a passionate channel for the voiceless and oppressed.

Yet in the midst of such angst and resignation, our vision of geo-justice is grounded in the understanding that the universe is predicated on and built for balance, for harmony, for interdependence—that is, for justice. Our work, then, is to align with that harmony, to change the ways in which we humans have interrupted the balance of the Earth's processes.

I approach geo-justice as a question to be lived. Like electricity, which we can only identify by its effects on other things—light bulbs and meters, stoves and motors, transistors, and electronics—I find it easiest to understand geo-justice by describing its effect on people caught by its vision.

Geo-justice is, in this sense, about liberating the Earth and its people from all oppression. This liberation unleashes our latent possibilities; our efforts become mini-Resurrections. These expressions of new life offer signs of hope within the events of our time.

Listening to these signs of hope, we are moved into action. Our responses call us into personal deaths—death to our isolation from self and from Earth; to a mechanistic worldview; to a tired understanding of justice that promotes resignation, despair, and misguided anger.

We mourn and lament the Earth's pain. We feel outrage at the violence inflicted upon our planet, as well as perpetrated by human upon human. At the same time, geo-justice invites us to undergo a profound shift of consciousness, to arise to a new resurrection moment. Resurrection is never about what was, but rather about what can be. It is always unexpected, always a surprise. The surprise of geo-justice is a new and expanded perspective on life. We discover delight in the rhythm of ocean waves, the caress of an evening breeze, the rich promise of a plowed field. Human life is part of a tapestry of gratitude—be it the support of a loved one, the urge for human rights, the joy of a newborn child, or the grace of racial and sexual equality.

At this crucial moment in the Earth's history, we are

invited to be collaborators, coworkers, and friends of the Earth. Thomas Berry says, "We are as much a part of Earth as the rocks, the water and the air." At certain times, we sense that unity with the Earth. The darkness of the sea, of the night sky, of our own soul—these are places where we feel ourselves hovering on the edge of new beginnings, new understandings, new responses.

In our moments of creativity, we know a unity with the world around us. We know that we belong to life in all its many manifestations. Instinctively, we reach for our origins, seeking our oneness with the Earth. Many years ago, I retraced the steps of my ancestors in southwestern and central Ontario, in Canada. I visited the farms, cemeteries, and remaining relatives of my French and Irish forebears. Traveling with my sister, I took from each grave site and farm a sample of the earth. At the end of the trip, I placed some of this soil in a small jar—which I still have—and labeled it "Jim's Bioregional Earth." Because that is, literally, the Earth from which I came.

We all come from the Earth. We who live on this planet are united in this *matter*—this mater, which is both Mother and Father—that is the unifying source of our being.

Our common heritage reminds us that we can be coworkers for geo-justice on our planet. In developing the concept of geo-justice, I find increasingly that geo-justice is about celebrating harmony and healing in and of the Earth. It is a holistic approach rooted in the Earth itself. Geo-justice seeks a resonance with the divine and with creation that will enable us to proceed further into this millennium and achieve a place of peace.

Geo-justice does not lend itself to the limits of a definition. Geo-justice is a vision, a language, a metaphor, an operative myth. It is an approach to healing the wounds of the Earth, a process for generating balance and harmony on the planet.

It operates through the healing energy of mysticism, and through prophetic work that both seeks and proclaims divine action in the world. As we discover our destiny, we are transformed. We see and act toward the Earth in a new way. Our energies attune to this work as a tuning fork sings when it picks up the vibrations around it.

Geo-justice reminds us that we *are* the Earth. We are not separate from the planet.

Like Little Children

Nothing illustrates better for me the nature of geo-justice than a young friend I had some years ago, named Julian. He was born in Honduras, a cradle of poverty and political strife, and then adopted by a Canadian couple. In their kitchen hung a plaque: "Never forget for a moment you didn't grow under my heart, but in it."

Julian never read Meister Eckhart, but as a child, his entire being declared Eckhart's theology: "The moment I flowed out from the Creator, all creatures stood up and shouted: 'Behold, here is God! They were correct.'"

Julian's approach to life was loving and inclusive. He celebrated every moment of his existence. I asked his mother what being his mother meant to her. "To understand the depth and joy of how he sees life," she replied. Julian was a child who saw every moment as an adventure. Whether it was a trip to the park, watching educational TV, or an encounter with his puppies, he greeted each option of living with ecstasy and engagement. He based his choices on a deep trust in his parents, his sister Laura, and those who delighted in who he was.

Julian celebrated the moment in un-self-conscious joy; he

allowed surprises to be part of his very being. He truly affirmed the gospel invitation to become as little children. His life was a constant invitation to be a child like him.

Julian taught me much about life. I thank him for being my teacher in geo-justice.

Becoming Shapers of the Future

Geo-justice starts with an awareness of the oppressed, the downtrodden, those in pain. It is an avenue of liberation for the voiceless and disempowered. Consider these words, for example, written by a federal prisoner in Ashland, Kentucky, during a retreat I conducted there. His poem reflects a deep appreciation of the creative energy that permeates all of life.

My dad was a violent man.
They told me I was a good boy.
When my father was not at home,
and when I was lonely,
I went out to see the stars and the moon.
And I wasn't lonely anymore.

In that retreat, I learned again that good things can happen in jail. Some of history's most powerful words have been written in prison—by Saint Paul, John of the Cross, Dietrich Bonhoeffer, Dr. Martin Luther King, Jr., Dorothy Day, Saul Alinsky, and others. In a sense, all of us are doing time in the cellblocks of our psyches and the confines of an oppressive culture. Geo-justice offers an avenue of liberation from those cellblocks for each of us.

When those inmates in Kentucky beat on drums together and ritualized their pain, a spiritual healing began. One inmate,

Tim, wrote a verse for the closing ritual: "And something came over me, and said I could be free." A few days later, he wrote me in a letter: "I have finished the day working in the aftermath of this weekend—I have found that since I slew my dragon, I am full of energy. I woke up to my spirit."

Tim recognized geo-justice as an awakening of the spirit, a discovery of our relationship with the cosmos, with people, and with God that liberates us from hopelessness and despair.

It was of this that the Trappist monk Thomas Merton said, "I exist under trees, I walk in the woods out of necessity. I am both a prisoner and an escaped prisoner. I cannot tell you why, born in France, my journey ended here in Kentucky. It makes no difference. Do I have a 'day'? Do I spend my 'day' in a 'place'? I know there are trees here. I know there are birds here... I share this particular place with them: we form an ecological balance."

From the perspective of geo-justice, the Earth can be seen as a balanced, living mandala, an integration of personal consciousness and global awareness. We re-vision justice making and become shapers of a future in which hope and compassion can replace abstraction and despair. We become aware that justice is ultimately the work of the universe. Our work is to become conscious participants in its ongoing unfolding.

The Power of the Universe

Deep within the recesses of our being, striving for expression, for recognition and strength, is a generative force. Often we do not know what to call it; we simply know it is there. Sometimes we become aware of it. Dr. Robert McClure, the Canadian medical missionary who served at great personal risk in four war zones, once described it as "a hand in the middle of your back, pushing you on."

This urgent force, once acknowledged, will not be denied. It cries out for expression. It demands release and liberation. From it arises a conviction that cannot to be held back. This force pays little attention to so-called common sense. It responds with compassion when it sees innocent children starving in Africa or hears teachers in the United States say that children in their classes regularly come to school hungry. It shows itself as fear in the wake of terrorist attacks in concert halls, movie theaters, classrooms, and offices. It rises in anger when unarmed Black men are gunned down by police in cities such Chicago, Cleveland, and St. Louis, or perhaps your town. It knows, beyond any argument or debate, that the world is not how it should be.

This profound and irrepressible generative force activates the latent strength of geo-justice. For if geo-justice concerns our oneness with the universe, then such a force can be nothing less than the power of the universe welling up within us.

Pope Francis tells us, "The intrinsic dignity of the world is thus compromised. When human beings fail to find their true place in this world, they misunderstand themselves and end up acting against themselves." It is only when we tap into the vision of geo-justice that we can begin to truly live.

The Invitation: Re-imagining the Lilies of Field

As the old order gives way, a new order is about to be born. What happened some twenty-one centuries ago is, I believe, deepening and expanding today.

At this time, our culture needs a hospice, a context in which old understandings and social structures can break down and die. At the same time, we need to be midwives to provide energy and support for the breakthrough of the new culture being born.

The movement toward breakthrough, toward becoming who we are, is for me very like spring. As René Dubos noted in *A God Within*, "To experience a spring day is enough to assure me that eventually life will triumph over death." Springtime bursts upon us with a new openness and invites us to participate in new life. Similarly, geo-justice invites us to participate in a new Earth. In geo-justice, we become instruments of planetary healing, connecting our own joy and pain to the Earth's.

It's a challenging position, walking on the hot coals of a dying culture even as we celebrate the first cries of new life. But that is what we are invited to do. The poet Barry Phillip (or BP, as he was called) Nichol was a friend to many and the catalyst of a group named the Four Horsemen, who performed their spoken-word poetry across Canada. One fall evening, I joined a group of about two hundred to celebrate the Canadian Thanksgiving. BP began to lead a haunting chant. The words "If we're here for anything at all, it's to take care of the Earth" echoed across the large room, which had once been a barn.

Similarly, the work of geo-justice invites us to our place on the planet. That birthright has deep roots in our tradition. It challenges us to deepen our awareness of our oneness with the Earth. Such an awareness will encourage concrete regional efforts and alternative strategies of healing. The healing will be a microcosm of the new world order to come.

Within the deepest recesses of our being, each of us carries a spark. That spark is a microcosm of the energy of the cosmos. I call this spark "soul" or "spirit." That spark is always new—it can erupt into flame unexpectedly. It is a reservoir of harmonious strength; it can fuel a relentless commitment. Like all fire, it is a source of energy. As a microcosm of the unfolding universe, it is always growing, always expanding, always in balance with the energy of the universe.

The work of geo-justice calls forth this spark in each of us. We are invited to an awakening awareness of the Earth and the cumulative events that move us inexorably toward the ongoing event of our day, a planetary Pentecost.

Within this context we can say:

- Each of us is invited to be participant and agent for weaving a tapestry of geo-justice, to be an instrument of harmony and balance for our planet.
- Each of us is invited to unity and oneness within ourselves, an adventure in global mysticism and peace.
- Each of us is invited to celebrate deeply the epiphanies of creation, discerned in the trajectory of each life.
- Each of us is invited to discover within ourselves what most ignites our psyche and connects us most profoundly to the journey of the cosmos.
- Each of us is invited to be a recipient of geo-justice in our own lives.
- Each of us is invited to co-create a planetary Pentecost for our time.

Process Reflection: I Have a Dream

One can discover a new incarnational moment with each hearing or reading of Dr. Martin Luther King Jr.'s famous "I Have a Dream" speech. In this chapter, I shared my own dream for the future. I invite you to do the same in this exercise, which is best done in a group, but can be done on your own.

1. One participant reads Dr. King's speech aloud. Alternatively, you can watch it on YouTube.

2. Everyone listens to the speech and reflects on it in silence.
3. Each participant completes the prompt "I have a dream …"
4. Participants are invited to read to the group the dream they have just composed.

Process Reflection: Letting Go of the Limited

Geo-justice offers an opportunity for letting go of the limited and opening to new vision. This exercise is best done in a group.

1. Begin by presenting images of the eyes of children.
2. Explain the challenge: to be people who see differently.
3. Each participant covers his or her eyes with a mask, or covers his or her head with a paper bag.
4. Each participant imagines a journey to a vantage point where he or she can "see forever."
5. When participants reach their imaginary vantage place, they pull off their masks and toss them away.
6. Each participant announces to the group what he or she is letting go of.
7. Together or individually, participants create a song, poem, dance, or prose expression of their understanding of a window for the world.

A Lesson of Solidarity

Hope comes from
listening to the Earth.
The Earth's story
teaches a lesson of solidarity.
The Earth's oppression is our own.
Listening in silence,
we become aware that we are not alone.
The joy of this realization
rescues us from loneliness
and connects us to the Earth.
In this connection,
we contact the divine.
We are both healers and healed.

Chapter 9
Cosmic Crucifixion: Dying as a Transforming Act

We cannot adequately combat environmental degradation unless we attend to causes related to human and social degradation.

—Pope Francis (*Laudato Si*, 48)

Pope Francis likes to relate a story that was told by a rabbi in the twelfth century. It harkens back to biblical times and the building of the Tower of Babel. The tower was made of bricks, and each brick had to be handmade. First the people had to make mud, and then they had to collect straw and mix it into the mud. Each brick was formed by hand, and then it was baked in an oven. Only after a brick was cold and hard could it be lifted into place at the top of the tower. Because it took so much effort, each brick was precious. If a brick fell and broke, it was considered a disaster, and the person who broke it was punished. However, if anyone fell from the tower and was injured or worse, there were no repercussions.

The pope concludes the story by saying that this kind of inverse priority is still happening today. If the value of a financial investment falls, it is considered a disaster. However, if people are hungry or sick or homeless, no one pays attention. This, says Pope Francis, is our crisis today.

We live in a culture where chasms divide us from ourselves, from each other, from the Earth, the universe, and the divine. A principal manifestation of this fragmentation is that more and more people experience a lack of tradition and of a unifying story. The societal urge to eliminate or ignore differences illustrates an illness that infects the soul of our culture.

The violence that is unleashed on minorities in North American cities confirms this cultural pathology. We are destroying the cities of this continent by propagating violence, crime, and death. The pervasiveness of this violence desensitizes us. The tremendous devastation around us seems to dwarf our capacity for constructive behavior and drain our hope.

The dream of growth and prosperity has failed. Industrialization and new technologies do not hold the answers for those who search for meaning. Progress has proven to be an inadequate panacea. The prosperity gospel, as preached by televangelist Joel Osteen and others, holds that financial success in this world is an indicator of eternal happiness in the next.

We are experiencing the ubiquity of the opaque dimension, and a dark night of our cultural soul. The United States is, among all nations, first in military spending (about 600 billion dollars a year), sixteenth in literacy, fiftieth in life expectancy, and twenty-sixth in infant mortality. At the same time, although this country only has five percent of the world's population, almost a quarter of the world's inmates are in U.S. prisons.

Destruction surrounds us. The human cost of greed is more than three billion people living in poverty, with about half of those living in extreme poverty. Every ten seconds, it is said, a child dies of hunger and malnutrition somewhere in the world. Every ten seconds! The regional and economic disparity, so prevalent on our planet, is powerfully portrayed in the following reflection by Art Laffin (2010):

> If the world were a global village of 100 people, five of them would live in the U.S. These five would have over one-fourth of the wealth, and the other ninety-

five people would subsist on the remaining three-fourths. How could these wealthy five live in peace with their neighbors? Surely they would be driven to arm themselves against the other 95—perhaps even to spend, as the United States does, as much on militarism as the rest of the world combined.

In our large urban centers, addiction, social conflict, unaffordable housing, homelessness, and unemployment are present every day. The daily litany of bias attacks and hate crimes—murders, rapes, bombings, and drive-by shootings—testifies to the deep cultural pathology that affects our cities.

Even the police, whose responsibility is to serve and protect, have been infected with our cultural love affair with violence, as seen in the epidemic of killings of young black men. Meanwhile, our legal system debates whether reasonable restrictions, such as background checks for purchasing weapons, would infringe upon our Second Amendment rights. When cops are killers, and all their bullets are legal, the outlook for order and justice is bleak indeed.

In the dominant culture, the poor and homeless are seen as problems to be solved, seldom as human beings with dignity and worth. We are often surprised when someone sees them as individuals. John Fitzgerald, an advocate for the homeless, tells a story about his first meeting with Dorothy Day, co-founder of the *Catholic Worker.* He was sitting in the Catholic Worker House on St. Joseph's Street in New York City. He waited patiently while she conversed with a drunken street woman. When they had finished their conversation, Dorothy approached John and said, "Did you wish to speak to one of us?" When John saw Dorothy viewing Christ in this homeless woman, he knew he was in the presence of a modern-day saint who could remind us that the divine is in our midst.

Distrust of Institutions

People no longer trust institutions. We live in an industrially advanced nation where workers can be fired at will—replaceable cogs in a corporate wheel. Even before the Great Recession, many workers were fired or laid off as a result of downsizing. Calling it "rightsizing" doesn't cushion the blow for the victims. If anything, it only emphasizes that the focus is on the corporations, not on the human beings who work for them. The corporations that decide the economic and personal fate of their employees tend to be governed by the bottom line. They function without accountability to their employees, or even to their shareholders. Corporate elites decide—behind closed doors—issues such as a just wage, fair profit, plant closures and relocation, and outsourcing. Choices are based on profit margin and marketing, not on families, futures, and years of dedication.

Education in many large cities is a custodial process whose product is, ironically, illiteracy. In Toronto and Chicago I learned firsthand that some high school graduates cannot read or write, which is news to no one. Inner-city transportation is expensive, inadequate, and unsafe. Negative economic incentives have driven people to unjust strategies for survival. The evidence that people have increasingly found themselves distrusting institutions is overwhelming.

Even the institutional church has come under suspicion. Although the Second Vatican Council gave birth to an understanding of the church as the People of God five decades ago, that vision did not survive in the years that followed. For many, the church seemed unwilling or unable to respond to the accelerated pace of our contemporary culture. Richard McBrien, theologian and author, suggested that many in the Catholic tradition have become "congregational Catholics," people who live their faith while disconnecting themselves from the structures of leadership that are so central to their experience of the church. Others have migrated to other denominations in an attempt to find faith without dogma.

Today, we are grateful that Pope Francis is engaged in revisioning the church as a place of love, meaning, and hospitality. He does not hesitate to speak out against corruption or to take to task those who have accepted kickbacks, saying that such people "have lost their dignity and give their children dirty bread." He likens this and other forms of corruption to an addiction, saying, "We might start with a small bribe, but it's like a drug," and he offers a prayer "that the Lord may change the hearts of those who worship the kickback god." Nevertheless, despite the pope's strong stance, I think it is fair to say that the days of unquestioning trust in the leadership of institutionalized church are over.

Distrust in the Political Arena

There is also intense mistrust in the political arena. More than half of those eligible to vote in off-year congressional elections don't vote, and less than sixty percent voted in the most recent presidential election. Further mistrust and anger arose after Hillary Clinton won the popular vote but did not win the election—the second time this has occurred in a presidential election in less than two decades. The widespread sense of disillusionment and lack of involvement in the political system can be understood as an echo of our alienation from the Earth.

We have inherited a frightening legacy from

industrialization and its false promises. Seeing the world as a machine, we have learned to treat nature and people as if they had no inherent value. This alienation from the Earth and from the political process shows up in unjust systems of oppression such as sexism, racism, classism. We desperately need to leave behind all these systems of control. We need to get off the ladder of domination and extend support and recognition to others— *all* others—and the entire Earth community. This journey is not an individual crusade. We need to join with others, seek a new perspective, and take action to revitalize our culture. We need one another in order to read the signs of the times and act to bring about justice and peace.

Knowing that democratic representation by elected officials has often been more symbolic than real enticed me to get involved in community organization. Properly developed, neighborhood organizations represent the interests of the community and engage local people directly in their own destiny. Over the years, I consistently sought cultural movements that promised a culture of life rather than the predictable, dominant culture of death. I was impressed by the vision of Senator Bernie Sanders, who ignited a fervent interest and new trust during the 2016 Democratic primary among groups, especially the young, who are outraged by the disparity between the billionaire class and the shrinking middle class, and who are alienated by the polarization of the political system.

To transform the roots of war, poverty, and ecological devastation we need to develop a more participatory democracy. The individual prophet must be replaced by prophetic communities. In the process of liberating our culture, we are called to heal both the biocide of the planet and the genocide of those who are considered other. We must become aware, as Alice Walker put it, that "when we cut the tree, our arm bleeds," and that no one is truly free until all are free.

The Illness of Cultural Collapse

By all accounts, we are unaware of the widespread pathology that has deeply infected us. One way to reflect on the current state of collapse is to compare it to an illness, such as cancer or a heart attack or alcoholism or the Ebola virus.

Physiologically, cancer is the runaway reproduction of cells in a biological organism. In Western civilization, we are afflicted with runaway consumerism.

This relentless growth pattern has produced overpopulated cities stifling in their own garbage all over the world. Our natural resources are being squandered, and disproportionately so. The average North American uses about 500 pounds of paper per year, compared to only about 16 pounds per person in Africa.

We have unleashed a vast devastation on the physical body of the Earth. Species are dying at an hourly rate. It is estimated that more than 150 acres of forest are destroyed each minute. Precious, irreplaceable topsoil is being washed into the sea—along with tons of pesticides—everywhere in the world.

The situation with water is equally if not more dire. The average American individual uses eighty-eight gallons of water a day, compared with about five gallons for an average African family. Notably, it takes 2,500 gallons of water to produce one pound of beef. Pope Francis reminds us that water is a lynchpin for geo-justice, saying, "Access to safe drinkable water is a basic and universal human right, since it is essential to human survival and, as such, is a condition for the exercise of other human rights."

Around the world, militarism and its inevitable partner, tyranny, proliferate out of control in country after country. Pollution chokes people who try to go outside in urban areas of China and India, and greenhouse gases circulate globally through the atmosphere, like leukemia in the bloodstream. From the dawn of the industrial revolution, smoke stacks have disgorged noxious gases into the atmosphere. Factories dump wastes into rivers and streams; automobiles gobble irreplaceable fossil fuels. In the name of progress, forests are denuded, lakes poisoned, and underground aquifers pumped dry. The Earth's occupants hover on the threshold of ecocide and genocide. Yes, the Earth has cancer.

Humans get heart attacks when their arteries are blocked by the fatty deposits resulting from over-rich living or when they live with chronically high levels of stress. The arteries in our bodies correspond to the dammed waterways of our streams and rivers, and the daily traffic jams of highways and airports. Ivan Illich said that it is difficult to explain to people from indigenous cultures why a machine designed to go 120 mph travels at no more than 15 mph in a twice-daily traffic jam. Automotive gridlock is a sign of our cultural cholesterol. In some cities, commuters spend up to the equivalent of two work weeks per year stuck in freeway traffic.

Our transportation arteries seem desperately in need of a bypass operation! But simply building more highways will not cure the illness.

Bodily illnesses require a change of lifestyle. So do cultural and ecological illnesses. If the healing of bodily ills is connected to a person's spiritual health, the healing of a culture depends on the awakening of a new consciousness.

And yet our governments and leaders, our industries and churches, continue to act as if these signs of devastation are not the most crucial issues of our lives. We pretend, as we go about business as usual, that someone sometime will solve the problems for us.

As with our personal illnesses, we first have to admit we are suffering. This is no small problem because most of us prefer to remain in denial. When we experience an issue in our family that terrifies us, we try to bury it. And if a family member draws our attention to it, we become angry. As we are confronted with the illness of our culture, we similarly deny it or become angry. But we need instead to name the crisis we live in and learn to respond in a healthy and effective manner. This is the only hope, whether on a personal or planetary level.

Once we have overcome our denial and anger—or skepticism—about the true state of our health, we face a far greater challenge: What can we do about the problem? How do we identify and then change those habits that have caused us to suffer such poor health, so much alienation and pain? There is no simple answer, but there is a place to begin.

We need to discover and embrace a spirituality of the Earth, to open ourselves not only to the crises of our times but also to the precious and stunning beauty of the Earth.

Our search is for something deeper than political ideas or economic policies; it reaches for a new way of life, one that flows out of an awareness of the cosmic story and the sacredness of the Earth. We need to change the habits that have made us so ill culturally and to discontinue the oppressive, addictive, and destructive behaviors we have perpetrated on our planet. In effect, we must liberate the physical Earth, and everything that lives on and in it, from those practices that cause it harm.

This challenge is enormous. Admittedly, it will be hard work and will take generations before we can say we have recovered. But we can and must begin. Then, out of our hope, we can move away from the destructive behaviors of the present. We can say we are in recovery.

When we reverence the Earth for its own sake, we create the possibility of prophetic cultural action. We have experienced what happens when the culture fails to understand the reality of the Earth's story: it becomes cut off from the people and planet. This cultural death is where we are now, facing the ruin and devastation of the planet. This watershed moment of cultural collapse awakens us to the opportunity for new understanding and healing.

The Voyage into Action

The pathology of contemporary culture springs, in part, from our resistance to accepting the basic dynamics of nature. When we embrace the natural order, we see that the human condition is not something separate from the natural world, but rather is intrinsically interwoven with the destiny and nature of the universe.

Gaining this awareness is not easy. We are surrounded with messages that praise bending nature to our will. I remember looking at a popular home improvement magazine. It presented three homes that had won awards for design and comfort. One of the three was in Arizona, and the article praised the builders for bringing a touch of their native Michigan to the desert. With massive irrigation, they had managed to create a green lawn surrounded by a white picket fence. The planet can ill afford this type of self-indulgence. It would have been better if the magazine had shown the beauty of a home that existed in harmony with its surroundings.

The divine is in every setting; we need to learn how to see it. Earth-centered education can open us to the news from planet Earth. When we acknowledge Earth as our primary classroom, we internalize the mystery of the natural world. We see the divine in our midst.

Today the stakes are high and the challenges great. As we survey the need for healing in our culture, the disparity we see between the depth of our insights and our capacity to translate them into action is an enormous challenge that brings a high degree of frustration.

There is so much need for change in our culture: war into peace, violence into justice, devastation into ecological balance, narcissism into cosmic consciousness, and gender inequality into opportunity for all. The opportunities that confront us are immense. The questions seem too big and too mysterious to be fully grasped. Our challenge is to live these questions with an open heart that is passionate, vulnerable, and joyful. We are confident that the questions contain within them the seeds of resolution. The paradox of death is that it can be seen as a transformative act. Pope Francis's words encourage us: "Together we must say no to hatred, no to revenge, and no to violence, particularly that violence which is perpetrated in the name of a religion or of God Himself.

Process Reflection: Making the Opaque Transparent

The mystery of evil is sometimes understood as an opaque dimension. Through reflection and compassionate action, we can make that dimension become more transparent; we can move from destruction to transformation. This exercise can be done alone or in a group.

1. The news from planet Earth reveals that we are living in the dark night of our cultural soul. How do you experience

the implications of this statement?

2. How do you understand the words of Ralph Waldo Emerson: "He has seen but half the Universe who has never been shown the house of Pain"?

3. In what ways do the new story of the universe and the practices of geo-justice and integral ecology empower you to deal with the bitter and burdensome dimensions of existence?

Canticle for Geo-Justice

Where there are ruptures in creation
we are aroused to peace.

Where there is disquietude
we are invited to balance.

Where there is discord
we are attuned to resonance.

In and through the pain of our wounded planet
we are called to make our Easter with Earth.

From collapse and devastation
we discover within the risen heart of the universe:
cosmic peace,
profound harmony,
deep balance,
compassionate resonance,
Pentecost for our planet,
geo-justice with Earth.

Chapter 10
Making Easter with the Earth: A Preferential Option

Let us be renewed by God's mercy ... and let us become agents of this mercy, channels through which God can water the earth, protect all creation and make justice and peace flourish.
—**Pope Francis** (Urbi et Orbi message, Easter March 31, 2013)

"Climate change is a global threat to security in the twenty-first century. We must act quickly to limit the future risks to the planet we share and to the peace we seek." In 2015, this challenge was posed by the European Union Institute for Security Studies in a report commissioned by the G7 countries.

In decades past, the threat of nuclear holocaust activated people to engage in the peace process. While that threat still exists, it has been superseded by an even more certain threat, that of ecological devastation. From this perspective, we could say the bomb has already begun to go off.

The signing of the Paris Agreement by 195 countries, as part of the United Nations Framework Convention on Climate Change in December 2015, gives us hope that this bomb can be stopped before it is too late. Although the agreement is non-binding—and as of this writing, may be overturned by the next U.S. president—it calls for each nation to commit to taking strong steps to reduce carbon emissions. Pope Francis expressed his pleasure with this show of action and urged the nations of the world "to carefully follow the road ahead, and with an ever-growing sense of solidarity."

More than ever, peace depends on our ability to achieve

a unity of purpose. Any meaningful vision of peace must first heal our separateness and energize a spirit of oneness. The illusion of separateness from self, each other, and creation must be dissolved. Our common connection to the Earth makes us all citizens of the same planet. This awareness of oneness with the planet allows healing responses to come forth.

In the prophetic words of Teilhard de Chardin, "The age of nations has passed. Now, unless we wish to perish, we must shake off our old prejudices and build the Earth." This emerging civilization must acknowledge differences without comparing them. It must value gifts without competing, and share a common vision of the future, as one family for a better world.

The experience of peace evokes gratitude for all of creation. Only in the absence of the aggression that has for so long permeated people, family, community, nation, and planet, we can show our reverence for the woods, the sea, the air as the sources of what is precious and important for life.

Solidarity with the Earth

As we have seen in the last couple of chapters, the tapestry of life, death, and rebirth is woven into each day, each individual life, and the destiny of Earth itself.

Pope Francis describes living the Paschal mystery at Easter as an opportunity "to go to meet others, to go towards the outskirts of existence, to be the first to take a step towards our brothers and our sisters, especially those who are the most distant, those who are forgotten, those who are most in need of understanding, comfort and help."

On one Easter, at Springbank Retreat in Kingstree, South Carolina, we were invited to share our stories of Easter. A woman rose and shared about another Easter morning when the congregation was gathering in silence for the liturgy. A young boy looked wide-eyed at the large cross with the corpus, and shouted exuberantly, "Jesus, what are you doing there? It's Easter. You're not dead anymore!" Amazement wafted across the congregation as the child's simple faith profoundly proclaimed the beauty and mystery of Easter to all assembled.

At some point in the unknown future, we will undergo physical death. As people of the Christian faith, we trust that life is changed at death, not ultimately ended. We believe that we are born again to eternal life. In this way, our own Easter follows that of Christ, who was born of Mary in the manger at Bethlehem, and then gave up his life on the cross at Calvary. Through the mystery of the empty tomb, he rose again and his cosmic presence found eternal life.

As people of geo-justice, we make our Easter with the Earth. We are as much of the Earth as are the rocks, water, and trees. We join with the Earth and all creation in this vast resurrection moment.

In our solidarity with the Earth, we know that we are born out of the dream of the divine imagination. Likewise, as inhabitants of this planet, we endure the inevitable burdens of life and all creation. The extinction of species, loss of top soil, clearcutting of forests, violation of the property and culture of native peoples at Standing Rock and elsewhere—these are the resurrection moments when self-healing properties become active among us, as we restore creation and restructure society and our lives.

Freire described his work of liberating the oppressed as "making my Easter." Similarly, the work of geo-justice involves making Easter by liberating every species, every human, and the Earth itself.

Geo-justice challenges us to a preferential option for the Earth. This option invites us into a practical solidarity with the wounds of the Earth. In the struggle for global justice, we view the planet itself as victim. The planet is hungry, sick, devastated, and dying. A preferential option for the Earth calls us to a theology rooted in the experience of global oppression; ecological devastation; and institutionalized resistance to social, gender, political, and economic equality. In solidarity, we see ourselves as part of the raped rainforests, abused children, marginalized peoples, and the economically disadvantaged. We embrace our experience of interconnectedness with the poor and with the poor Earth. We awaken to the needs of the biosphere.

This solidarity, in turn, helps us discover that the needs of the Earth are one with our own deepest desires. That is the source of what I called magnetic intuition. Thus, a preferential option for the Earth honors the impulse to integrate the rhythm of our lives with the processes of the planet itself.

Peace with the Earth

Matthew Fox tells us, "Peace on earth cannot happen without peace with the earth and peace among all earth creatures." Some characteristics of that peace are:

- Democracy, participation in a dignified manner with all life forms
- Disarmament, the acknowledgment of the basic needs of all expressions of life
- Tolerance, the acknowledgment of our essential equality
- The emergence of the divine feminine, which manifests

in inclusiveness and collaborative leadership
- Protection for the oceans, the very source of emergent life
- Protection against deforestation, a compassionate response to the life systems of the environment, the very lungs of this Earth
- Promotion of mental health and psychic balance for people on the planet to make drug addiction obsolete

In these characteristics, sociology and ecology merge. New structures of global responsibility restore harmony between people and nature. A better world will be built out of mutual sensitivity and vulnerability.

The Earth was not created for people, but people were created for the Earth. You have probably heard the saying "Think globally and act locally." Robert Muller, who was Assistant Secretary-General of the United Nations for forty years, rephrased that as "We need to think cosmologically, and act globally and locally."

Our cooperative actions, though diverse in expression, will send ripples for peace throughout the planet. Out of a sense of responsibility for a peaceful future, we will celebrate the sacredness of all life. A Bri Bri native teacher of Costa Rica proclaimed this truth: "We share the same sky, same sun, same river; we are all one."

Understanding this unity calls forth an awareness of our common roots and of the presence of the divine in all things. We see that all humans must share in healing our current sense of separateness from the Earth.

As people of peace, our commitment to this time is to make wisdom possible, to experience love and beauty, to participate in the unfolding consciousness of the planet as a living being.

In this period of extraordinary change, we celebrate that everything is part of everything else on the Earth.

So we search for a strategy to help us move from ambivalence to ecological commitment. We seek a strategy that is effective, liberating, and appropriate for the magnitude of the issues that confront us. The fact that an increasing number of people share this view provides encouragement.

Energy for planetary peace will be focused through participation in our local communities. Through the practices of liberation theology in Latin America, and contextual theology in South Africa, such communities have been the means of revitalizing the local culture. They will do the same for peace with the Earth.

As communities collaborate, a growing number of peacemakers will discover increased harmony within and balance without. Because the local communities will be inclusive and non-hierarchical, cultures of violence will change to nonviolence.

The Rights of the Earth

Peace is an essential dimension of geo-justice. Peacemakers take it upon themselves to remain open to life and available to surprise. They receive everything as given, and trust the giver. They express their interdependence with all that they receive. They see and celebrate peace with the Earth as a gift of geo-justice.

My friend Joanna Macy is an example of a peacemaker. The emphasis of her work shifted from the nuclear crisis to the ecological crisis. When she visited the areas of Russia contaminated by the Chernobyl disaster, she was moved by a story she heard there. Immediately after the disaster, when winds would have carried the radioactive material to Moscow, the government made the decision to seed the clouds so it would fall instead on a less populated area. When Joanna gave her workshops in this area, she taught the people to do an Elm Dance. By honoring the trees for absorbing the radiation and silently suffering alongside the people, this ritual generated a powerful healing energy. With this attitude, peace is possible and geo-justice is alive among us.

Geo-justice is not a single program that others must follow. Rather, it celebrates and depends on the diversity of each of our expressions of healing and compassion.

Geo-justice draws together a coalition of people sharing a common vision, working out day by day a new configuration of energy for our culture, our planet, and ourselves. This coalition finds its focus in the image of roots and wings. Roots invite us to mine our traditions and our origins, to find within them the stories and the strengths that keep us going even when success seems unattainable. Wings summon us to soar, to see visions and dream dreams, to seek personal and political frontiers as yet unattained.

To participate in such a coalition, our unique contribution to geo-justice must start with who we are and what we do right now. Our surrounding mainstream culture, like a computer, strives to program every action and direction of our lives. It is willing to shape us to what we are not. By being and acting who we are, we are liberated from this oppression.

Geo-justice is about healing the separation in our lives and on the Earth. We have too much separation—between personal and political, body and body politic, generativity and the ability to act, mysticism and global perspectives, prophecy and local action, self-knowledge and social awareness. Coming together to build a communal spirit will move us toward the global event, a planetary Pentecost, the advent of a new kind of healing.

Geo-justice is an expression of vision, a process of healing the Earth. With this vision, we see the Earth and life in a new way. We have a new perspective, a new window for the world.

The action that flows from this perspective is the work of geo-justice.

Process Reflection: Your Contribution

Pope Francis says, "I ask you to be builders of the world, to work for a better world." And he more specifically says, "I would like to ask all those who have positions of responsibility in economic, political and social life, and all men and women of goodwill: let us be 'protectors' of creation, protectors of God's plan inscribed in nature, protectors of one another and of the environment." Geo-justice is fully participatory. This exercise can be done alone or in a group.

1. Brainstorm a list of what interests you most about geo-justice.
2. What contributions do you think you might make to geo-justice?
3. Who are your geo-justice role models?
4. Choose the contributions that most appeal to you. Develop priorities and strategies. Try to identify some long-term strategies, and some that you can implement almost immediately.
5. From the many possibilities that emerge, decide what is most important. Make a commitment to do it.

Process Reflection: How I Would Like to Be Remembered

In the heat of daily life, we don't always maintain perspective on our contributions to the greater whole. We lose sight of our highest aspirations and most cherished goals. This exercise is best done in a group, but can be done alone, as well.

1. Participants gather in a circle.
2. As the participants relax, the leader invites them to go back to their childhood years and remember what they wanted to accomplish with their lives, and then to think of what they now want to do with their remaining days.
3. With a background of soft instrumental music, participants are asked to complete the sentence "I would like to be remembered...."
4. After writing down their answers, participants choose a partner and share what they have written.
5. Finally, the participants gather in a large circle and each partner reads aloud his or her partner's statement to the group.

At the Feet of the Cosmos

Strong forces,
somehow at play,
unleash newfound hope
of integration.

Long years of division
slowly knitting
into a painful combination
of love and letting go.

Doubts and aspirations fly by
in successive bursts,
inviting a new perspective on life.

Search for self gives way
to a growing cosmic awareness,
a quickening grasp
of who we could be.

Ocean and mountains beckon,
a silent invitation
from the strong and relentless forces
of Earth's energetic way.

To sit at the feet of the cosmos,
bidden by those majestic forces
that speak the Earth's wisdom—
this untracked route
somehow I must go.

Chapter 11
The Emergence of a Planetary Pentecost: Healing the Earth

We cannot become starched Christians, those over-educated Christians who speak of theological matters as they calmly sip their tea. No! We must become courageous Christians and go in search of the people who are the very flesh of Christ, those who are the flesh of Christ!
> —**Pope Francis** (Pentecost Vigil, Saint Peter's Square, May, 18, 2013)

Pentecost reminds me of walking home at dusk in my small Ontario hometown. When the street lights went on, I suddenly could see those whom I would meet.

Pentecost happens whenever "the lights go on," whenever people realize they are not walking alone. Whenever I invite people at a geo-justice seminar to find someone they don't know and to share what is important to them, they almost always report a wonderful experience of interconnectedness with the other person. This healing of separation is Pentecost.

Musically, harmony involves blending individual notes into a common chord. Science teaches us that the universe is a symphony of harmony and balance. This offers an auditory image of Pentecost. Often, in geo-justice groups, I ask each person to hum a particular note. Research indicates that the Earth vibrates at C-sharp. When we all hum C-sharp, we are not only in resonance with each other but with the Earth, as well. The resulting sound reminds us powerfully of unity and peace.

A Planetary Earthquake

We are being called by the pain of the Earth to be architects of the new era that lies ahead.

As our capacity to know the planet as a whole increases, we share a collective consciousness through which the Earth becomes aware of and reflects upon itself. The new understanding of our origins—through art, science, and mysticism—has released an enormous energy and interest among a growing number of people pursuing a spirituality of the Earth.

This cultural earthquake marks the end of an era. Until now, our value system has operated on "more and better," on compulsion and competition. These values are exemplified in large urban centers. Gentrification drives out large numbers of people; the result is increased homelessness, with city people becoming urban refugees. As this homelessness occurs more broadly upon the Earth, we have environmental refugees.

Many people today are experiencing personal crises. These crises, in many ways, parallel the planetary earthquake that is upon us. They are reminders that the divine energy of the universe sometimes calls us to change our patterns of living and being. Properly understood, a crisis becomes an opportunity. A crisis can launch each of us into the work of personal and social transformation, with global consequences. We have a fresh chance to realign our lives with our true vocation and purpose. This change is like altering a sailboat's course to compensate for a changing wind.

As long as we resist or block the cosmic truth of our lives, the crisis intensifies. This condition seems to me like a kind of psychic colitis. When disruptive health patterns constrict its proper function, the colon rebels. In the same way, when we constrict the flow of divine energy in our lives, our very beings rebel. Seeing crisis as an opportunity for breakthrough enables us to become more open to our true destiny. We can experience life as more pleasurable, profound, meaningful, and compassionate.

Redirecting our lives brings great joy, but is often accompanied by pain. Any change involves breaking down ingrained patterns of thought and living and creating new ones. But despite the pain of change, the subsequent shift makes it increasingly possible to savor life's greatest gifts and achieve harmony in our lives. We become an expression of the geo-justice that we are invited to create.

Pain and Paradox

We live today in a time of great pain. Our cities are wracked with senseless violence. Our rivers are poisoned, our oceans are dying. Our atmosphere chokes on greenhouse gases. More than at any other time in the past twenty centuries, the Earth reflects Paul's words to the Romans: "The whole creation has been groaning as in the pains of childbirth."

Paradoxically, this pain carries great hope for a planetary Pentecost, a new way of living together on the planet. The problems are all related; so are the solutions. Just as in that moment at dusk when the street lights are turned on and the darkness of isolation ends, we can now see everything as interconnected, woven together.

Meister Eckhart reminds us that the work of transformation is whatever needs to be done within the world around us: "One who truly has God will have Him in all places, in the streets and in the world, no less than in the church." Transformation is not only a response to the demands of the task at hand, it is best accomplished by someone who is open and committed to personal change.

Personal transformation can happen when we fall in love. When we fall in love with a person, we find ways to be with that person, even if it means changing many aspects of our lives. We can also fall in love with a place, an ocean, a cause, or an idea, among other things. This attraction opens us to beauty. It dissolves the barriers, internal and external, separating us from it. It is truly transformative, for nothing remains the same.

Personal transformation can also occur through a breakdown of some sort. In that breakdown, internally trapped energy is released and can become the fuel for personal transformation. We let go of some things that oppressed us, and accept the need to change. Our society is at present going through something akin to a nervous breakdown. We need to let go of some attitudes, suppositions, and systems that were once considered essential.

In geo-justice, we recognize anew our capacity to be instruments of healing and justice. An awareness of our personal pain, united with the pain of the Earth, becomes a basis for our work. By getting in touch with our pain for the outrage perpetrated on the Earth, we generate energy to throw off the blanket of inertia that stifles creative action and that promotes resignation and despair.

We feel freed to act, at our own level, in our own situation. As we act, we participate in healing the Earth. If we allow the pain we feel to be simply personal, it can be limiting, separating, and isolating. Geo-justice challenges us to move to a more expanded level. It is an important moment for the Earth and for ourselves.

Geo-justice emerges from the dynamic of the Earth itself. The process is geological, biological, and human. It invites a reflection on the role of people within the universe. It reminds us to let go of domination and move toward participation in the harmony already present in the universe. Geo-justice depends less on us being initiators than on us being participants, members of the gigantic chorus that flows into all aspects of existence. Geo-justice finds expression in the equity and relationship of all creation.

Now, in the twenty-first century, we imagine new ways of taking responsibility for our life and for the world, for living out our preferential option for the Earth. We re-vision ways to restructure society and to transform the various forms of oppression that we experience. Geo-justice invites us to be people of justice; instruments of harmony; participants in balance; promoters of interconnectivity; and healers of the ruptures in the fabric of creation that cause injustice for the psyche, society, and the planet.

When we get in touch with our deepest convictions and find them congruent with the roots of our faith, we can generate a genuine enthusiasm for life and a preferential option for the Earth.

The key to Pentecost is an awakening from our depths. A planetary Pentecost is the expansion of this healing moment for the Earth in our time. It affirms life and confirms the goodness of the Earth.

The planetary perspective makes possible a vision that takes us beyond ourselves to see the world in a new way. Healing the Earth will also heal us.

A Place to Stand

The movement toward geo-justice is shaped by the context in which it occurs. For example, geo-justice in Latin America is not the same as in North America. Because different regions liberate and oppress the Earth in different ways, each must respond differently.

We live in an important time—a time of hope, of struggle, and of geo-justice. We live in a time when the dominant culture and some dimensions of organized religion militate against justice and change. We live in a time when religious language can be put to the service of the status quo, when a disembodied spirituality can subtly oppress people and justify the unjust. Never has the call to work and destiny been so much a call to geo-justice.

A primary goal of life is to discover our place, our role. We want to fulfill our potential; we want to make a significant contribution to life on this planet. This is usually best accomplished by living out what we *feel*, rather than what we *think*. Our minds can be easily misled by argument; our instincts are rarely swayed by rationalizations.

When we explore the patterns of the past, we usually find that our lives have not proceeded linearly like train tracks. A friend used to tell me: "Don't follow someone else's path. Go your own way and leave a trail." When we listen to and act on our deepest feelings, we are putting down our own tracks, creating our own futures, declaring that our lives are in our own hands. We are not trapped into conformity; our values are not limited to survival and domination where we always have to be right and others wrong.

Archimedes illustrated this capacity to create our own future: "Give me a place to stand and a lever long enough, and I will move the world."

Pope Francis shows us that we can move the world in large and small ways. When he was visiting Philadelphia, the Pope was in his car when he spotted a young boy with cerebral palsy. His car stopped and he got out and went over to the boy and kissed and blessed him. On another occasion, a mother whose child has cerebral palsy reached out to the Pope, asking for his blessing. Some time later, the telephone in their small apartment rang. The mother answered and she heard a voice say, "Good morning, this is Pope Francis." He was calling to speak with her son, Michael. Later, the boy said he was feeling better and that he felt "like somebody important." He also said, "I will do what the Pope asked me to do: I will pray for him."

Each of us, from wherever we stand, can contribute our energy toward the transformation of the planet. This is geo-justice making, the fulfillment of our destiny.

When we truly move toward transformation, we are in touch with our dreams and connected to our visions. Dreams retrieve from the unconscious the energetic and archetypal sources of our lives, which have both global and personal significance. Visions help us to sketch, as it were, the painting that has not yet been put on canvas. They reveal options and possibilities; they animate practical action. They provide revelatory moments. Dreams and visions are the internal events, activities, and indicators that point us toward our participation in the life of our planet.

If emotional turbulence results from this new involvement, we can best handle it by allowing it to surface, to be experienced. We continue to focus energy on the task at hand, the work of transformation; we see the emotional experience as fuel for our work.

The Time is Now

Although it's not possible to see into the future, we do have to make decisions in the work of geo-justice. Under the constraints of schedules, time frames, and other commitments, many choices present themselves. Fear and indecision are predictable, but decisions must be made.

We need to draw on as many vehicles as possible for gaining insight into our world. No source of knowledge is out of bounds, no access to mystery and the sacred need escape us. Neither psychology nor scripture, tarot nor tradition, reading our palms or reading the stars can provide all the answers for us. We are responsible for discovering our own calling, for living our own life, for choosing our own place in the work of geo-justice.

Our work is to bring harmony, balance, and peace to the planet. Whatever the focus of our individual work, the most important dimension is that we see our efforts within a larger context of interconnected energies acting as one huge transformer, illuminating and awakening the entire Earth. This is the planetary Pentecost.

As we contemplate our future, we realize that a new moment is upon us. We stand on the threshold of a new beginning. The doorway of opportunity challenges us to be workers for a planetary Pentecost, to animate the energy necessary to move us into the future. A Paschal moment of death and rebirth summons us.

To what?

To a bright future, filled with promise, rising from a
dangerous past
To a time of hope, rising from despair
To a time of mystery, rising from a fixed and frozen now
To a time of participation, rising from a passive
observation of life
To a time of adventurous self-understanding, rising from

an armored resistance
To a time of global concern for our endangered Earth,
rising from a time of privatized domination
To a time of integration and tenderness toward the Earth,
rising from extinction, waste, and planetary poison
To a time of global consciousness, rising from our
fragmented psyches
To a time for geo-justice, rising from the resources and
legacies of those who have gone before

Those who have labored long to build the Earth are being
rediscovered, and others are awakening to the need. Within
the collective unconscious of the culture, the awareness that
our primary concern is the Earth is evolving. We are moving
toward a turning point, a convergence of awareness and action.
We are here to heal the planet.

Process Reflection: Interconnectedness

In this group exercise, the woven yarn becomes a metaphor for
the web of cosmic fire that connects us and that constitutes the
work of geo-justice on the planet.

1. Form a circle of participants.
2. Distribute balls of different colored yarn to each person.
3. Invite people to hold the end of the yarn, and throw the
   balls to each other.
4. Participants observe as a web of many colors forms.
5. Finally, participants share their reflections on equality and
   interconnectedness, as generated by this exercise.

Process Reflection: A Litany for Transformation

One response to the questions of birth and death is to compose a litany, a poetic form of prayer in which one's petition to God typically uses repetition. This exercise can be done alone.

1. In the litany that follows, I first offer what needs to be born (the Resurrection component) and then I can see what needs to die (the cross dimension) before the Resurrection can happen. I have arranged these antiphonally, to emphasize the possibilities of breakthrough embodied in this cultural moment.

   Trust needs to be born,
   Security needs to die;
   Liberation needs to be born.
   Oppression needs to die;
   Celebration needs to be born.
   Boredom needs to die;
   Connectedness needs to be born.
   Alienation needs to die;
   Global awareness needs to be born,
   Nation-state-ism needs to die;
   Creativity and courage need to be born,
   Fear of death needs to die.

   The right brain needs to be born,
   the left brain needs to be happy about it;
   feminism needs to be born,
   patriarchy needs to die;
   soul-making needs to be born,
   individualism needs to die;
   recovery needs to be born,

addiction needs to die;
playing together needs to be born,
competing needs to die;
the ecological age needs to be born,
environmental genocide needs to die;
reverence for all life needs to be born,
domination and objectification need to die;
doing-with needs to be born,
doing-for needs to die;
be-attitude needs to be born,
have-attitude needs to die.

Hope needs to be born,
despair needs to die;
creative silence needs to be born,
empty noise needs to die;
awareness needs to be born,
insensitivity needs to die;
circles need to be born,
hierarchies need to die;
dialectic needs to be born,
dualism needs to die;
laughter and tears need to be born,
sadness and sentimentality need to die;
a new order of geo-justice needs to be born,
the old order needs to die.

2. Create your own litany of actions and concerns that matter
   to you.

Emergence

When hopes seem dashed,
and faith diminished,
when all we thought was promised
begins to dissolve and shatter before us,
we descend to the floorboard of our souls.

There, caught in the turbulence of the moment,
we search for the still point of the sacred.
In that place of uncertainty,
we open to the unexpected,
welcome the possibility of the new.

PART IV
Walking the Path of Integral Ecology

Chapter 12
Signposts of Geo-Justice

The natural environment is closely related to the social, political, and economic environment. It is urgent for all of us to lay the foundations for an integral ecology—this is a question of health—an integral ecology capable of respecting all these human dimensions in resolving the grave social and environmental issues of our time.
—**Pope Francis** (*Care for Creation*, 2016, p. 80)

Albert Nolan, a theologian and colleague of Nelson Mandala, writes, "It is by reading the signs of our times that we discover what kind of time we are living in." Justice making flows out of reading the signs of the times, out of seeing in trends and countertrends what is going on. Until we know that, we cannot decide what needs to happen and what we are willing to take responsibility for changing.

When we fail to read the signs of the times, we are condemned to continue in old patterns. The first step in geo-justice is a willingness to break with past patterns. Geo-justice does not deal with an ideal or abstracted world; it starts where we are, right now. The healing of the Earth and its people begins as a response to the cultural moment in which we are living.

Three Signposts

Three signposts can help us discern how we might participate in the work of geo-justice. These three are planet, place, and path. They can perhaps be best recognized in three questions.

1. "What are my roots?" (my relationship to the planet)
2. "What is my work in geo-justice?" (my place)
3. "Who am I?" (my path)

In seeking answers to the questions that represent planet, place, and path, we recognize that we ourselves are a microcosm of the cosmos we attempt to nurture. In this way, we view the psyche, and the whole human organism, within the context of the culture and the universe. We have a direction; we are going somewhere. We are an arrow toward the future. Focusing on planet, place, and path helps us challenge our present perceptions, collapse stereotypes of self, and move beyond the present toward the future.

People everywhere are searching for responses to these questions. One person I think of is a musician. As a child, he felt called to the religious life. However, his nature was not compatible with life in an institutional structure, so he did other things. Later in life, he rediscovered his calling through a passion for music, and now he makes and sells his music. In a sense, I see him as an archetype of those who are exploring new approaches to what Thomas Berry would call their "great work." They know that they may not find final answers to their questions, but they celebrate revelatory moments and palpable instants of contact with the divine, as their lives unfold.

As Thomas Merton said, "If I never become what I am meant to be, but always remain what I am not, I shall spend eternity contradicting myself by being at once something and nothing."

For all of these people, a profound sense of homecoming (planet), compassion (place), and spirituality (path), identify their motivation.

Homecoming

This planet is our home. We have no other home. But vast numbers of people have no sense of the Earth as their home. Lacking roots, they have no sense of true homecoming.

Years ago, while I was a student at the Canadian Urban Training Project, I worked with the rootlessness of single displaced men who came to the Fred Victor Mission in Toronto's inner city. Wandering the streets myself on an urban "plunge," I shared their experience of homelessness. I realized for the first time how homelessness has turned city dwellers into urban refugees, people who live in cardboard condos. Unlike the rest of us, they have no home to return to each night.

We all need a home. Our homecoming, in this sense, is about returning to our origins, to celebrate our roots. Not just to come home to the farms where our ancestors once lived, but to come home to the universe, to the Earth, to our culture, our traditions, and ourselves—and to accept all of this as home.

Homecoming celebrates the interconnectedness of all reality. It is a spirituality of "Aha!"—a sometimes startling recognition of who we are and where we have come from. We belong. We feel a comfortable congruence of our life with the life of the planet, an experience of peace that provides the security to free us from clinging to past practices.

Homecoming recognizes that we came from the Earth, are of the Earth, and will return to the Earth. We reclaim our origins, our starting point. And each time we go back to that starting point, we begin again. So our work in geo-justice is always new.

Compassion

Henri Nouwen said that we are called to recognize the sufferings of our time in our own hearts, and to make that recognition the starting point of our service. Our service, he said, "will not be perceived as authentic unless it comes from a heart wounded by the suffering about which [it] speaks."

This concept of the wounded healer empowers a compassionate response. Our wounds are not just our own—they are also the wounds of the Earth. When we explore our pain, we discover where our strength and our freedom are, and where justice lies. Understanding the deep connection between our personal pain and cosmic pain, we feel the urgency of taking action to heal the Earth.

Our current cultural and ecological crises show us the futility of resolving our personal problems at the expense of others or of the environment. The most appropriate energy for our work is that which brings healing to both ourselves and society.

Our woundedness indicates our capacity for compassion in a wounded world. Our pain and the pain of the planet are catalysts to work toward oneness in the universe. In the work of geo-justice, we "atone" for the past—that is, we make ourselves "at one" with the cosmos. Our vulnerability to the pain of the Earth, like a psychic compass, guides our destiny. We are motivated not only by our sensitivity to the suffering of others, but also by an overarching vision of how the world could be. Acting out of compassion, we find our place as we seek to heal the wounds of the Earth.

Spirituality

Spirituality moves us beyond concerns of career and ambition to a continuing process of change. Spirituality allows us to understand the world we live in. It is essentially our "take" on the meaning and purpose of our lives. We could say our spirituality provides our pilgrimage through life.

Spirituality is an awakening to the depths of who we are, an unfolding of our own story. It generates an understanding of ourselves and the Earth. It affirms connections between the universe and the culture. We engage fully in the here and now, without regretting the past or fearing the future. The experiences of our lives are the context in which we discover our path to our place on the planet.

We can only know what we're supposed to be by awakening to what we already are in the depths of our own souls. Brian Swimme says of that awakening: "If we pursue these paths, our lives—even should they become filled with suffering and hardship—are filled as well with the quality of effortlessness."

Spirituality speaks of our souls. Therefore it speaks deeply to our experience. An integral spirituality will not invite us to withdraw. Rather, it invites us into life as an unlimited possibility. It offers hope, opportunity, possibility, and future.

For the new era of global interdependence, we need a mature spirituality that reverences creation for its own sake, a spirituality that understands our perception of creation through the senses as an experience of the divine. We need to be able to deal with social structures as well as personal attitudes, with multinational corporations as well as family life. For we are dealing here with our whole civilization, our whole planet.

This is a transformative path. Its wisdom shows us how to live in resonance with the Earth. Teilhard de Chardin summarized this approach: "I became aware that I was losing contact with myself. At each step of the descent, a new person was disclosed within me of whose name I was no longer sure and who no longer obeyed me. And when I had to stop my exploration because the path faded beneath my steps, I found a bottomless abyss at my feet, and out of it came—arising I know not from which—the current I dare to call my life."

Each person who is on a spiritual journey is called to make sense of uncertainty. We are challenged to recognize the mystery that is spirituality, and that guides us in the ongoing discovery of who we are and what we are meant to be.

The Quest for Geo-Justice

We live in ominous and foreboding times. When we read the signs of the times, we see our nation and others around the world caught up in deepening political unrest. Many groups feel compelled to oppose their own best interests. The polar ice caps are melting. Young black men are being shot in the streets. First nation people are struggling to preserve their culture and protect their land. The Paris Agreement designed to reduce the carbon footprint on the planet is in jeopardy. These and other signs of the times challenge us to an extent that the current generation has not been challenged before.

Of course, this is not the first time our world has faced the threat of totalitarianism or fascist tendencies taking hold in the hearts and minds of people. Wars have been fought; millions have lost their lives. Thankfully, if we look to history, we can find instances when we pulled back from the brink and democracy prevailed. One example that comes to mind is the diplomacy engaged in by President John F. Kennedy during the Cuban missile crisis in 1962 that deterred the possibility of a nuclear holocaust following the disastrous Bay of Pigs invasion. Today, in our quest for geo-justice, we and the rest of humanity have choices to make and paths to carve out if we are to preserve our way of life, and even life itself.

As we become aware of the signs of the times, many around the country are gathering in living rooms, on street corners, and online to tell our stories. We are doing our best to listen and respond to the cry of the poor and the cry the Earth. We are attempting to trace and understand the sequence of events that led us to this day. We hear the call to enter an era of heroic times, as expressed by the prophetic voice of Thomas Berry. He urges us not to accept a world of aggression and exploitation, but to choose hope, mercy, justice, peace, democracy, and ultimately a path toward the dawn of a new and wondrous day.

Reading the signs of the times may appear to forebode a dark and doomed future, but I believe those signs also reveal the unfolding presence of the divine in our midst. A better future can only be born from envisioning the planet in new ways: of being, of relating, of dreaming, of building community, of nurturing our spiritual vision, of questing for our collective soul.

There will be signs to assure us we are on the right path. As we enter a new era, and geo-justice moves from our psyches to the structures of our land, we will witness a new civilization emerging.

Process Reflection: Following the Signposts

In the quest for geo-justice, the following questions stand as signposts representing our concerns with planet, place, and path. You can respond to them in a group or on your own. Come back to them after some time has passed and see how your answers have evolved.

1. How do we go about building new structures, new forms and ways of doing things, new centers of energy for a cultural genesis in our day?
2. How do we change things without repeating the tyrannies of our present culture, even if it is for a different cause? Where do we start?
3. How do we build mediating institutions between the powerful structures of greed that dominate our lives and the gentler forms designed for nurture? How, in fact, do we nurture the structures that nurture?
4. How can we bring about a consciousness of geo-justice, an awakening to the mysticism that emerges from the depths of our awareness?
5. What do you think needs to be born and what needs to die?

Process Reflection: Walk the Labyrinth

A labyrinth is a powerful tool for reflection. It is a symbol for the spiritual journey that has been used over the centuries. If you know of a labyrinth near your home, go there and walk it. Otherwise, you can create a simple one in a small space.

1. Research online to find a labyrinth design you want to create. Websites you might consult include https://labyrinthsociety.org/, http://www.labyrinthos.net and many others
2. You can create a labyrinth outside using stones in the woods or on a beach, using sticks on a lawn, or chalk on pavement. You can create one inside using masking tape

on a floor.

When you are ready to walk the labyrinth, take a minute to prepare yourself. Clear your mind before you start. You may want to hold an intention or question or prayer in your heart, focusing on something you would like to learn from this act of reflection. The Springbank Retreat divides a labyrinth walk into three steps:

3. Walk slowly in silence toward the center. This step represents a letting go or releasing of your worries and worldly concerns so you can be open to receive when you reach the center.
4. At the center, stop and reflect. The center is a place for prayer and meditation. As you rest there, allow yourself to receive greater clarity about your life.
5. As you walk away from the center, carry with you what you have just learned. In one way or another, you have touched the divine mystery. Now you can bring that back with you into your life.

Wait

Inspired by each movement of the spirit
that stirs us deeply,
we sink below the turbulence
and pay attention to the promptings of the heart.
Enveloped in the gaze of Jesus,
preoccupations and plans melt away.
In and through this intimate approach,
we surrender to the ever-present now,
and undefended before our loving God
in silent expectation,
we listen for the voice that calls us forward.

Chapter 13
The Gospel of the Moment Process

A great cultural, spiritual, and educational challenge stands before us and it will demand that we set out on the long path of renewal.

—Pope Francis (*Laudato Si'*, 2012)

As I reflect on geo-justice at this particular moment in history, in light of a disastrous election that signaled increased peril for our fragile planet, I choose to hold fast to the vision that a promising future awaits us. I refuse to relinquish hope.

Reflecting on the legacy of his country, German theologian Johannes Metz wrote, "For me, doing theology meant doing theology in the face of Auschwitz, in the face of the Holocaust. And though this holds good in a very special way for Christians and theologians in Germany, it does not apply to them exclusively, for the Holocaust is not just a German catastrophe, but on closer inspection, a Christian catastrophe. I began to ask myself: 'What sort of theology can one do with one's back to Auschwitz—before the impending catastrophe, during the catastrophe, after the catastrophe of Auschwitz.'" In the same way, today we cannot do geo-justice and integral ecology with our backs to the current turbulence and threats to our basic democratic values and the well-being of our planet.

The gospel of the moment calls upon us to both read scripture and to be aware of the state of the world and to respond in a reflective and transformative way. This gospel of the moment process begins with a community of self-aware people who hold an evolutionary worldview in which each person wakes up to an entirely new world each day. It is a world in which we pursue our true destiny. Empowered by companionship and the ability to act, we move forward to more fully realize what is possible.

A New Era of Engagement

As we internalize the gospel of the moment and extend compassionate action to the poor and suffering, the least, the lost and left behind, we awaken to a new opportunity. Our response will be prompted by an enhanced sensitivity that extends to self, other, Earth, and God. It will be signified by widening compassion as we respond to the needs of all members of our planetary community.

Through contemplation, liberation, and creation-centered engagements, we will witness the unlocked power of each person, connect the stars to the street, and inaugurate the work of geo-justice.

Our new engagement will allow us to stand up to abusive power at the same time that it inspires courage, creativity, and hope. In circles of solidarity, we imagine a better future, and as W. E. B. Dubois phrased it, "respond to the mighty causes that call us." Each person's narrative of engagement will embrace faith and be transformed in a new world of love and social solidarity. We discover the strength to "put feet into prayer" and move forward with inspiration and a new energy.

We listen to the echoes of the liberating mantra "Let my people go" and move from being victims to being heroes. We are energized to build a new Noah's ark, a cultural context constructed by acts of hope, service, and justice. The new ark will be a place to travel together into a more promising and fruitful future. We will experience homecoming in a revolution inspired by Francis of Assisi, who proclaimed, "Preach the gospel at all times. If necessary, use words."

The practice of geo-justice involves self-discovery. It will include coming home to a rootedness in our spiritual tradition enhanced by various wisdom sources. It will heal alienation and support an integration of inner work and actions to heal the people and the planet.

This great work will remove the distance modern technology often places between ourselves and those we are called to serve and encounter. It will heal the culture that tolerates religion without transcendence, art without beauty, education without character, and law without justice.

As we replace fear with love, and broken heartedness with relationship, we see again, like the astronauts, a whole and healthy planet, the Earth seen from outer space. As we reach out beyond our comfort zones and areas of influence, we are guided by the words of Dr. Martin Luther King, Jr.: "Justice at its best is love correcting everything that stands against love."

With this perspective in mind, we can awaken from the psychic numbness that paralyzes our culture. We can discover the power surging through the universe that is available in our spiritual traditions and to each of us today.

A Sheaf of Spiritual Practices

There is no blueprint for fashioning geo-justice, as one might put together a child's wagon. However, I am convinced that a collective vision of geo-justice is indeed emerging from our cultural crises, from the beauty and pain of the Earth. We are being invited to discover and articulate that vision.

Breaking out of predictability, we engage in a dialogue with all creation. We pursue an Earth-centered approach to compassion. We integrate theology and experience, relationships and spirituality, roots and innovation, lifestyle and conviction.

In this dialogue, we remain open to questions and to surprise. We affirm that we are more than our brokenness. We acknowledge the deep wisdom that is nourished by silence, fueled by moral outrage and energized by a profound trust in life's unfolding. Moving toward both autonomy and interconnectedness, we experience a self-direction that demonstrates hope and trust in our inner voice, leading us into a life yet unborn. This self-direction finds its basis in the land, its vision in an unfolding future, and its energy in the moment we are about to live.

There are some specific things we can do to put together a framework of practices to animate our work of geo-justice. For example, here are some things you could do that I, or members of my classes or workshops, have done.

- Spend 15 minutes a day in nature, reading the primary scripture of the cosmos
- Spend time with children and animals
- Experience deeply and ritualize each of the seasons
- Savor and celebrate the four elements in your life: earth, air, fire, and water
- Gratefully bless your food and remember the Earth as its source
- Develop art-full living through painting, clay, poetry, and music
- Practice storytelling, listening, ritual, and celebration
- Explore in groups the divine language of dreams
- Participate in sports that are not competitive
- Practice Thomas Berry's commandments of creation: "You shall remove all poison from the air.

You shall cease all pollution of the water.
You shall be open to the life-giving radiance of the sun.
You shall support the self-sustaining forces of the universe."

I invite you to add your own practices to these suggestions.

Participating in the Gospel of the Moment Process

I have designed a gospel of the moment process that can be used with small groups, based on the work of Paulo Freire. Over the years, I have conducted various participatory experiences, but this format represents a synthesis of all my ideas. In essence, a collective awareness of the gospel of the moment can be achieved through a five-fold process: a descriptive phase, the generation of themes, an interpretive phase, an action phase, and finally theological reflection.

The descriptive phase. The process begins with the formation of small groups, or learning circles, each with four to eight participants. However, you can follow a similar process on your own if a group is not available.

Members of the learning circle are first invited to reflect on their life experience and write down several things they view as obstacles that hold them back. They are asked to give concrete examples of why they are not free to be the person they long to be. For example, participants might come up with the following list:

- Financial problems, such as affordable housing, unemployment, low wages
- Pain, illness, or other health issues

- Relationship challenges, such as loneliness or domestic violence
- Lack of meaning and purpose in life

Second, they are asked to reflect on and write down several obstacles they see as standing in the way of a flourishing society and healthy planet. For example, they might list the following societal and ecological obstacles:

- Violence, including mass shootings and other gun deaths
- Intolerance and hatred, including terror attacks and racism
- Political corruption
- Climate change, including refugees, flooding, and starvation
- Inequality

Clustering experiences into generative themes. When members of each small group have completed their lists of obstacles, they are invited to share with other members of the group.

Following this sharing, the members of the group are asked to look at all their lists together and begin to cluster the results under common themes.

Typically, this process yields five or six common themes. These themes can reflect both personal and societal/ecological obstacles. However, a group may choose to focus on one or the other, depending on the commonalities in their individual lists.

Examples of generative themes that followed from the obstacles listed in the first phase include:

- We experience stress when we feel we can't control vital aspects of our lives.
- We experience alienation when we don't connect with our community.
- We feel powerless because change is not happening as fast as we want.
- The Earth is the victim of excessive human greed.
- Our environment will not support life if we don't clean it up.

The action phase. In this phase, participants identify one or more actions to which they commit, based on the generative themes they have identified and the codes they have created. Examples of actions that might follow from the themes and codes listed here include:

- Volunteering one afternoon a week at a community shelter
- Participating in a political campaign or local grassroots action group
- Giving away personal items, such as clothing, that have not been used in over a year
- Committing to carpooling

Theological reflection. An important dimension of being empowered by our critical reflection to engage in acts of transformation is founded on a conviction that flows from a faith perspective. Therefore the gospel of the moment process ends with a phase of theological reflection.

Questions to conclude the gospel of the moment process include:

- How does this theme and the proposed response—
  personal and collective—either affirm, change, or
  contradict your worldview and faith tradition?
- How are you able to reconcile what you intuitively
  and instinctively experience as true with what you
  currently hold as true as received from your inherited
  faith tradition?
- Name the strategies and action that underline your
  engagement in the world and describe how these are
  supported by your worldview and faith tradition.

To Ignite a True Future

People of a common story, we are bound together in a
compassionate embrace. We follow the vision of Thomas Berry,
who wrote about the original flaring forth that ignited our
psychic energies and about how we have been shaped and fired
in the same primordial furnace.

As we ignite our sense of the future, we ponder the origin
of the universe and the transformational events that have led to
this present moment. It is a narrative replete with mystery and
meaning, and an awareness that consciousness has been there
from the very beginning and is present in each of us from our
earliest moment of life.

We embrace the vision of Teilhard de Chardin, who
blended Christianity with evolutionary principles. The
question we inevitably ask is "What are we going to be and do
next?" As we move forward into the next wave of evolution, we
echo the wisdom of Teilhard, who proclaimed, "I am a pilgrim
of the future on my way back from a journey made entirely in
the past."

Thus, we take our place as a people paused on the doorway

of new beginnings. We are fueled by the enduring impulse to become creators of a new story. This story emerges from the embers of an energy that ignited our imaginations in the past and whose sustaining force remains with us today. It is a renaissance of energy. A psychic spark was ignited in our soul, and from that time on, a new door has been open to the future. We know that tomorrow will be different from today, that we can be delivered to ourselves, that we can break free from the dramas of everyday existence and discover our true destiny.

We remember the counsel of Meister Eckhart, who said that after a breakthrough, "we may return to the stable." He reminds us that the deepest transformations in our lives are not necessarily accompanied by external manifestations. The return to the stable, the reentering of involvement in daily life, can also be an affirmation that our breakthrough was an authentic spiritual experience. The most authentic expression of geo-justice lies in who we are, not in what we do.

Our existence is punctuated by the joys and sorrows that prepare each new tomorrow as an opportunity to reach out courageously into the future. After all, we know—in the words of Saul Alinsky—that we're "never going to go back anyway." In our ongoing journey, we retrieve each new moment as a chance to act freely and gain access to what remains to be discovered—an engagement that nourishes and transforms. With each passing day, we celebrate the sacredness of a life-enhancing unfolding and meet the future that is struggling to be born.

We listen to the sacred voice summoning us to life and reminding us that integral ecology means our commitment to the natural world cannot be indifferent to social justice. We must embrace each new tomorrow with a holistic understanding that encompasses both beauty as well crises in an inclusive synthesis. We are called forward into a new planetary challenge that invites us to navigate the turbulent waters of contemporary culture and recommit ourselves to fall in love with the dream of a better tomorrow. Together, we fashion this new tomorrow so we can become more alive to nature, culture, and ourselves.

As we look to the future, we stand at a crossroads between suicide and exaltation. We are poised to celebrate the emergence of a joyful integral ecology that promises a new era in which we discover what it means to be human and to participate in a vast evolutionary event.

We pray that our country rises to a better day, infused with the hope and trust of those who join us on the way. Each time a person stands up for an ideal or seeks to improve the lot of others or strikes out against injustice, he or she sends forth a tiny ripple of hope. And that ripple, combined with a myriad others, can sweep down even the mightiest walls of oppression and injustice.

Process Reflection: Participating in Geo-justice

Geo-justice is a participatory journey. I encourage you to reflect on the emergence of integral ecology and put your reflections into action. I leave you with three reflections to guide your journey in geo-justice.

1. How can continuing education, social media, and group dialogue become expressions of justice making?
2. What vehicles are available to you in your life for the practice of geo-justice?
3. How can mysticism, prophecy, and self-discovery enable you to participate in the practice of geo-justice?

Praise to All Creation

Praise be to you, O God.
I hear St. Francis say,
Praise be to the water, sunshine, and rain.
Praise be to you, all children of the world.
From deep within the deserts of the Earth,
I hear the cry:
Quench my thirst.
Heal my heart.
Bless my soul.
Every place where withinness lies,
may hope flow into love
and become a world of happiness.
Amen.

Bibliography

Alinsky, Saul D. *Reveille for Radicals*. New York: Random House, 1946/2010.

——. *Rules for Radicals: A Practical Primer for Realistic Radicals*. New York: Random House, 1971.

Andrus, Marc, and Matthew Fox. *Stations of the Cosmic Christ*. San Francisco: Tayen Lane, 2016.

Baum, Gregory. *Compassion and Solidarity: The Church for Others*. Toronto: House of Anansi Press, 2006.

——. *Man Becoming: God in Secular Experience*. New York: Herder and Herder, 1970.

Berry, Thomas. *The Christian Future and the Fate of Earth*. Maryknoll, NY: Orbis Books, 2011.

——. *Creative Energy: Bearing Witness for the Earth*. San Francisco: Sierra Club Books, 1996.

——. *The Dream of the Earth*. New York: Random House, 1988.

——. *Evening Thoughts: Reflecting on Earth as Sacred Community*. Edited by Mary Evelyn Tucker. San Francisco: Sierra Club Books, 2006.

——. *The Great Work: Our Way into the Future*. New York: Bell Tower, 1999.

Berry, Thomas, and Thomas Clarke. *Befriending the Earth: A Theology of Reconciliation between Humans and the Earth*. Mystic, CT: Twenty-Third Publications, 1991.

Boff, Leonardo. *Church: Charism and Power: Liberation Theology and the Institutional Church*. Translated by John W. Diercksmeier. Eugene, OR: Wipf and Stock, 2012.

——. *Cry of the Earth, Cry of the Poor*. Maryknoll, NY: Orbis Books, 1997.

————. *Toward an Eco-Spirituality*. New York: Crossroad, 2015.

Boff, Leonardo, and Dinah Livingstone. *Francis of Rome and Francis of Assisi: A New Springtime for the Church.* Maryknoll, NY: Orbis Books, 2014.

Brockelman, Paul. *Cosmology and Creation: The Spiritual Significance of Contemporary Cosmology.* New York: Oxford University Press, 1999.

Busch, Vincent. *The Creation Mandala*. Quezon City, Philippines: Claretian Publications, 2004.

Carlson, Rachel. *Silent Spring*. Boston: Houghton Mifflin, 1962/2002.

Casey, Michael. *I Was There: The Universe Story for Children 8-80*. Dublin: Danann, 2015.

Conlon, James. *At the Edge of Our Longing: Unspoken Hunger for Sacredness and Depth.* Mystic, CT: Twenty-Third Publications, 2004.

————. *Becoming Planetary People: Celebrations of Earth, Art and Spirit.* Union, NJ: Trowbridge & Tintera, 2016.

————. *Beauty, Wonder and Belonging: A Book of Hours for the Monastery of the Cosmos.* Lima, OH: Wyndham Hall, 2009, 2013.

————. *Earth Story, Sacred Story*. Mystic, CT: Twenty-Third Publications, 1994.

————. *From the Stars to the Street: Engaged Wisdom for a Brokenhearted World.* Toronto: Novalis Press, 2008.

————. *Geo-Justice: A Preferential Option for the Earth.* Winfield, BC: Wood Lake Books, 1990.

————. *Invisible Excursions: A Compass for the Journey.* Lima, OH: Wyndham Hall, 2012.

————. *Lyrics for Re-Creation: Language for the Music of the Universe.* New York: Continuum, 1997.

————. *Ponderings from the Precipice: Soulwork for a New Millennium*. Leavenworth, KS: Forest of Peace, 1998.

————. *Sacred Butterflies: Poems, Prayers and Practices*. Lima, OH: Wyndham Hall Press, 2013.

————. *The Sacred Impulse: A Planetary Spirituality of Heart and Fire*. New York: Crossroad, 2000.

de Chardin, Pierre Teilhard. The Divine Milieu. New York: Harper, 2001.

————. *The Human Phenomenon*. Translated and edited by Sarah Appleton-Weber, Portland, OR: Sussex Academic Press, 2003.

Delio, Ilia. *The Emergent Christ*. Maryknoll, NY: Orbis Books, 2011.

————, ed. *From Teilhard to Omega: Co-creating an Unfinished Universe*. Maryknoll, NY: Orbis Books, 2014.

————, ed. *Personal Transformation and a New Creation: The Spiritual Revolution of Beatrice Bruteau*. Maryknoll, NY: Orbis Books, 2016.

————. *The Unbearable Wholeness of Being: God, Evolution and the Power of Love*. Maryknoll, NY: Orbis Books, 2013.

Dubos, René J. *A God Within*. New York: Scribners, 1972.

Fiand, Barbara. *Come, Drink Deep of Living Waters: Faith Seeking Understanding in the Twenty-First Century*. New York: Crossroad, 2016.

Finks, P. David. *The Radical Vision of Saul Alinsky*. New York: Paulist Press, 1984.

Fox, Matthew, *The Coming of the Cosmic Christ: The Healing of Mother Earth and the Birth of a Global Renaissance*. San Francisco: HarperSanFrancisco, 1988.

————, ed. *Meditations with Meister Eckhart*. Santa Fe, New Mexico: Bear, 1983.

————. *Original Blessing: Primer in Creation Spirituality.* Santa Fe: Bear, 1987.

————. *The Reinvention of Work: A New Vision of Livelihood for Our Time.* San Francisco: HarperSanFrancisco, 1995.

Fox, Warwick. *Toward a Transpersonal Ecology: Developing New Foundations for Environmentalism.* Boston: Shambhala, 1990.

Francis, Pope. *Care for Creation: A Call for Ecological Conversion.* Edited by Giuliano Vigini. Maryknoll, NY: Orbis, 2016.

————. *The Church of Mercy.* Chicago: Loyola Press, 2014.

————. *The Joy of the Gospel: Evangelii Gaudium.* New York: Random House, 2014.

————. *Laudato Si': On Care for Our Common Home.* Huntington, IN: Our Sunday Visitor, 2015.

————. *The Name of God is Mercy Treatise.* Raleigh, NC: Lulu Press, 2017.

————. *The Simple Wisdom of Pope Francis: The Joy of Evangelization.* Washington DC: United States Conference of Catholic Bishops. 2013.

Freire, Paulo. *Pedagogy of Freedom: Ethics, Democracy, and Civic Courage.* New York: Rowman & Littlefield Publishers, 1998.

Gebara, Evone. *Longing for Running Water: Ecofeminism and Liberation.* Minneapolis: Augsburg Fortress, 1999.

Grim, John, and Mary Evelyn Tucker. *Ecology and Religion.* Washington DC: Island Press, 2014.

Grof, Stanislav, ed. *Ancient Wisdom and Modern Science.* Albany, NY: State University of New York Press, 1984.

————. *Beyond the Brain: Birth, Death, and Transcendence*

in Psychotherapy. Albany, NY: State University of New York Press, 1985.

Gutierrez, Gustavo. *We Drink From Our Own Wells: The Spiritual Journey of a People*. Maryknoll, NY: Orbis, 1985/2013.

Haight, Roger. *Jesus, Symbol of God*. Maryknoll, NY: Orbis Books, 2000.

Hanh, Thich Nhat. *Interbeing: Fourteen Guidelines for Engaged Buddhism*. Berkeley, CA: Parallax Press, 1987.

Haught, John F. *God after Darwin: A Theology of Evolution*. Boulder, CO: Westview Press, 2001.

————. *Resting on the Future: Catholic Theology for an Unfinished Universe*. New York: Bloomsbury, 2015.

Horton, Myles, and Paulo Freire. *We Make the Road by Walking: Conversations on Education and Social Change*. Edited by Brenda Bell, John Gaventa, and John Peters. Philadelphia: Temple University Press, 1990.

Johnson, Elizabeth A. *Ask the Beasts: Darwin and the God of Love*. London: Continuum, 2015.

————. *Friends of God and Prophets: A Feminist Theological Reading of the Communion of Saints*. New York: Continuum, 1998.

————. *Quest for the Living God: Mapping Frontiers in the Theology of God*. New York: Continuum, 2007.

————. *The Strength of Her Witness: Jesus Christ in the Global Voices of Women*. Maryknoll, NY: Orbis Books, 2016.

King, Ursula. *Christ in All Things: Exploring Spirituality with Teilhard de Chardin*. 2nd ed. Maryknoll, NY: Orbis Books, 2016.

————. *Spirit of Fire: The Life and Vision of Teilhard de Chardin*. Maryknoll, NY: Orbis Books, 2015.

Laffin, Arthur J. *Swords into Plowshares: Volume Two: A Chronology of Plowshares Disarmament Actions, 1980-2003*. Eugene, OR: Wipf and Stock, 2010.

Lasch, Christopher. *The Culture of Narcissism: American Life in an Age of Diminishing Expectations*. New York: W.W. Norton, 1991.

Lesser, Elizabeth. *The Seeker's Guide: Making Your Life a Spiritual Adventure*. New York: Random House, 2000.

Lonergan, Anne, and Caroline Richards, ed. *Thomas Berry and the New Cosmology*. Mystic, CT: Twenty-Third Publications, 1987.

Macy, Joanna, and Molly Young Brown. *Coming Back to Life: The Updated Guide to the Work that Reconnects*. Canada: New Society Publishers, 2014.

Macy, Joanna, and Chris Johnstone. *Active Hope: How to Face the Mess We're In without Going Crazy*. Novato, Calif.: New World Library, 2012.

Martin, James, ed. *How Can I Find God?: The Famous and the Not-So-Famous Consider the Quintessential Question*. Liguori, MO: Liguori/Triumph, 1997.

———. *Jesus: A Pilgrimage. New York*: HarperCollins Publishers, 2014.

McDonagh, Sean. *To Care for the Earth: A Call to a New Theology*. Santa Fe: Bear, 1987.

———. *Climate Change: The Challenge to All of Us*. Dublin: Columba Press, 2006.

———. *The Death of Life: The Horror of Extinction*. Dublin: Columba Press, 2004.

———. *The Greening of the Church*. Maryknoll, NY: Orbis Books, 1990.

———, ed. *Reflections on Laudato Si'*. Dublin: Veritas, 2017.

McFague, Sallie. *The Body of God: An Ecological Theology*.
    Minneapolis: Fortress Press, 1993.
McLuhan, Marshall. *Understanding Media: The Extensions of
    Man*. Cambridge, MA: MIT Press, 1994.
Merton, Thomas. *When the Trees Say Nothing: Writings on
    Nature*. Edited by Kathleen Deignan. Notre Dame, IN:
    Sorin Books, 2003.
Metz, Johannes B. *Poverty to Spirit*. Mahwah, NY: Paulist
    Press, 1968.
Moore, Thomas. *Care of the Soul: A Guide for Cultivating
    Depth and Sacredness in Everyday Life*. New York:
    HarperCollins, 1994.
———. *Original Self: Living with Paradox and
    Originality*. New York: HarperCollins, 2000.
———. *A Religion of One's Own: A Guide to Creating a
    Personal Spirituality in a Secular World*. New York: Avery,
    2015.
Nolan, Albert. *God in South Africa: The Challenge of the
    Gospel*. Grand Rapids, MI: Eerdmans, 1988.
———. *Hope in an Age of Despair: And Other Talks and
    Writings*. Maryknoll, NY: Orbis Books, 2009.
———. *Jesus Today: A Spirituality of Radical Freedom*.
    Maryknoll, NY: Orbis Books, 2006.
Nouwen, Henri J. *The Wounded Healer: Ministry in
    Contemporary Society*. New York: Doubleday 1972.
O'Donohue, John. *Anam Cara: A Book of Celtic Wisdom*. New
    York: HarperCollins, 1997.
———. *Eternal Echoes: Exploring Our Yearning to Belong*.
    New York: HarperCollins, 1999.
O'Murchu, Diarmuid. *Ancestral Grace: Meeting God in Our
    Human Story*. Maryknoll, N.Y.: Orbis Books, 2008.
———. *Evolutionary Faith: Rediscovering God in Our*

Great Story. Maryknoll, NY: Orbis Books, 2002.

———. *Quantum Theology: Spiritual Implications of the New Physics*. New York: Crossroad, 1998.

O'Sullivan, Edmund. *Transformative Learning: Educational Vision for the Twenty-First Century*. New York: Zed Books, 1999.

Palmer, Parker J. *Let Your Life Speak: Listening for the Voice of Vocation*. San Francisco: Jossey-Bass, 1999.

Raymond, June, ed. *Meditations with Thomas Berry*. London: GreenSpirit, 2010.

Richards, M.C. *Centering in Pottery, Poetry, and the Person*. Middletown, CT: Wesleyan University Press, 1964.

Ruether, Rosemary Radford. *Gaia and God: An Ecofeminist Theology of Earth Healing*. San Francisco: HarperSanFrancisco, 1992.

Scharper, Stephen Bede. *Redeeming the Time: A Political Theology of the Environment*. New York: Continuum, 1997.

Some, Malidoma Patrice. *The Healing Wisdom of Africa: Finding Life Purpose through Nature, Ritual and Community*. New York: Putnam, 1999.

Steindl-Rast, David. *The Way of Silence: Engaging the Sacred in Daily Life*. Edited by Alicia von Stamwitz. Cincinnati: Franciscan Media, 2016.

Swimme, Brian. *The Universe Is a Green Dragon: A Cosmic Creation Story*. Santa Fe, New Mexico: Bear, 1984.

Swimme, Brian, and Mary Evelyn Tucker. *Journey of the Universe*. New Haven: Yale University Press, 2011.

Swimme, Brian, and Thomas Berry. *The Universe Story*. San Francisco: HarperSanFrancisco, 1992.

Taylor, Barbara Brown. *The Luminous Web: Essays on Science and Religion*. Lanham, MD: Rowman & Littlefield, 2000.

Toben, Carolyn W. *Recovering a Sense of the Sacred: Conversations with Thomas Berry.* Whitsett, NC: Timberlake Earth Sanctuary Press, 2012.

Uhlein, Gabriele, ed. *Meditations with Hildegard of Bingen.* Rochester, VT: Bear, 1983.

Wallis, Jim. *The Soul of Politics: A Practical and Prophetic Vision for Change.* New York: The New Press, 2006.

Wheatley, Margaret. *Leadership and the New Science: Learning about Organization from an Orderly Universe.* San Francisco: Berrett-Koehler, 1992.

Whyte, David. *The House of Belonging.* Langley, WA: Many Rivers Press, 1997.

Winter, Miriam Therese. *The Singer and the Song: An Autobiography of the Spirit.* Maryknoll, NY: Orbis Books, 1999.

Acknowledgments

I express my gratitude to John Tintera and Katharine Carroll for bringing this project to print, and to Jude Berman and Marilyn Goddard for their assistance in preparing the manuscript.

About the Author

Jim Conlon was born in Canada in 1936. He received a degree in chemistry from Assumption University of Windsor, and later in theology from the University of Western Ontario, and a PhD from Union Institute and Graduate School. Deeply moved by the impact of the second Vatican Council, the civil rights movement, and the Vietnam War, Jim moved from pastoral work to the streets. Today he is one of the leading teachers of the new narrative of the cosmos. Visit him online at www.jimconlon.net and on Facebook at www.facebook.com/becomingplanetarypeople.

Also by Jim Conlon

Becoming Planetary People
Celebrations of Earth, Art & Spirit
ISBN: 978-0-9964387-0-4

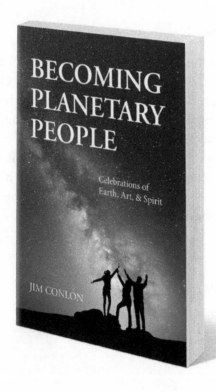